A PENTECOSTAL APPROACH to BIBLE STUDY

James

A PATH TO DISCIPLESHIP

DISCOVERY GUIDE

ISBN: 978-1-940682-09-9

Table of Contents

Foreword

May God's peace and power be yours! By selecting this Bible Study on James, you have already demonstrated your passion for spiritual growth. You are also to be commended for making a good choice. James is passionate about discipleship! Like the prophets of old, the Epistle of James is a call for genuine spiritual change in the Lord. This call is not for the fainthearted! From the very first verse of his epistle to the last word of one of the most stirring doxologies in all of Scripture, James expects great things of those who take God seriously. Yet the rewards of humble obedience to the message of James are enormous. It can be said without hesitation that anyone who hears the voice of God in James and makes a personal covenant to obey God's voice will never be the same again.

So you are about to be "drawn into" (the true meaning of *inductive*) one of the most exciting and life-changing studies of God's Word. It will be a journey of discovery and life-giving challenges at every turn, for James serves as a "roadmap" for authentic spiritual formation. The "vehicle" that will move you toward your spiritual goals is a twelve-week inductive study of the Epistle of James. During the first week, the leader of your group will share from the *A Pentecostal Approach to Bible Study*. This important work will teach you what inductive Bible study is (from henceforth IBS) and how to use this exciting method for yourself. The content of *A Pentecostal Approach to Bible Study* is essential for successfully completing this *Discovery Guide*. On the other hand, if you want to study *James: A Path to Discipleship* on your own, you can read *A Pentecostal Approach to Bible Study* for yourself. This Bible study can be obtained from Church of God Adult Discipleship, or Pathway Press.

Once you have reviewed the material in *A Pentecostal Approach to Bible Study*, you will begin the IBS lessons contained in this *Discovery Guide*. Each lesson will cover about half of a chapter in James. Thus the five chapters of James will consist of ten carefully crafted IBS lessons—each designed to be completed in one week. During these ten weeks, you will be called upon to develop creative tools for interpreting the Bible and will be invited to pray for a new work of God to occur in your life. You will also compose your own spiritual journal to track your progress and to retain a record of your commitments to God and the Bible. And James wouldn't be James if you were not challenged to take real action and do what the Word of God says. Yet most importantly, you will quickly be immersed in the Bible and be empowered to learn God's Word on your own.

The twelfth and final week will be a wrap-up session that, once again, will be directed by your IBS group leader. During this lesson, you should be prepared to share all of the exciting truths that you have learned from your study on James. And again, if you are studying *James: A Path to Discipleship* on your own, you should take this last week to prayerfully review all that God has spoken to you through His Word. It is just this kind of reflection that makes IBS such a powerful tool of discipleship. The goal of IBS is not just to learn facts about God's Word, but to be spiritually transformed through God's Word.

So in the spirit of James, the time for talking is over. It is time to take action!

William A. Simmons, Ph.D.

LESSON ONE

James

1:1-12

REAL FAITH
IS MATURE, INSIGHTFUL, AND STABLE

Lᴇssᴏɴ Oɴᴇ
James 1:1-12
Real Faith Is Mature, Insightful, and Stable

 ## Kᴇʏ Vᴇʀsᴇ

If any of you lacks wisdom, he should ask God, who gives generously to all without finding fault, and it will be given to him (James 1:5).

Introduction

Congratulations! Now that you have reviewed the book *A Pentecostal Approach to Bible Study* which explains how to do an inductive Bible study, you are now prepared for an exciting journey of discovery in the Epistle of James. Throughout this study you will apply all of the "Helping Questions" (five W's and one H: Who? What? When? Where? Why? and How?) and devise a number of "Helping Tools" (symbols, highlighting, etc.) to help you uncover God's truth for yourself. Don't worry; this *Discovery Guide* will supply plenty of structure to guide you on your way. However, active, hands-on learning is a hallmark of IBS. As you work through this guide you will create your own tools for studying God's Word. In this way you will end up with a personalized study of the Epistle of James that will prove to be more fun and memorable than if you simply reviewed someone else's work.

The format for this study on James will be as follows: The lesson will begin with a copy of the text to be studied for that week. You will notice that plenty of room has been left between each line. This space is for you to write in notes, symbols, and marks as you work through the lesson. Then the four D's of inductive study (**Discover . . . Discern . . . Devote . . . Disciple**) will serve as "signposts" on your *Path to Discipleship*, that is, your very own study of the Epistle of James. Always keep in mind that as you come to know James better by way of the **Discover** and **Discern** steps, the goal of your study is to be spiritually transformed through the **Devote** and **Disciple** steps. Indeed, the last step (**Disciple**) is the most important part of your work! As you become discipled *in* the Word, you are now to go out and make disciples *by* the Word (Matt. 28:18-20).

All of this means that sincere prayer and sensitivity to the Spirit are vital for truly understanding the Bible. With that in mind, it's time to get started!

PAUSE *for* 🙏 PRAYER

There can be no true understanding of God's Word apart from prayer. This is why the apostle Paul interceded on behalf of the Ephesians. He prayed: "I keep asking that the God of our Lord Jesus Christ, the glorious Father, may give you the Spirit of wisdom and revelation, so that you may know him better. I pray also that the eyes of your heart may be enlightened in order that you may know the hope to which he has called you, the riches of his glorious inheritance in the saints" (Eph. 1:17-18).

Take a moment and ask God to give you "the Spirit of wisdom and revelation" as you study through this lesson. Pray that "the eyes of your heart may be enlightened" as you study this wonderful Epistle of James. And finally, pray that "you may know the hope to which he has called you" so that you can press on to that full and mature knowledge of the Bible.

 # THE TEXT

James 1:1-12

[1]James, a servant of God and of the Lord Jesus Christ, to the twelve tribes scattered among the nations:

Greetings. [2] Consider it pure joy, my brothers, whenever you face trials of many kinds, [3] because you know that the testing of your faith develops perseverance. [4] Perseverance must finish its work so that you may be mature and complete, not lacking anything. [5] If any of you lacks wisdom, he should ask God, who gives generously to all without finding fault, and it will be given to him. [6] But when he asks, he must believe and not doubt, because he who doubts is like a wave of the sea, blown and tossed by the wind. [7] That man should not think he will receive anything from the Lord; [8] he is a double-minded man, unstable in all he does. [9] The brother in humble circumstances ought to take pride in his high position. [10] But the one who is rich should take pride in his low position, because he will pass away like a wild flower. [11] For the sun rises with scorching heat and withers the plant; its blossom falls and its beauty is destroyed. In the same way, the rich man will fade away even while he goes about his business. [12] Blessed is the man who perseveres under trial, because when he has stood the test, he will receive the crown of life that God has promised to those who love him.

DISCOVER

The primary task of this step of IBS is to "*dis*-cover" the truths in God's Word. In fact, the word "*discover*" comes from the Greek word *apocalupsis,* which literally means "to unveil" or "to reveal." It is from this word that we get the name of the last book of the Bible, the Book of Revelation. So first, carefully read James 1:1-12 . . . then . . . read it again. This is to be an *active* reading whereby you pull out relevant data from the text. Here you are to *observe* all of the key words and facts contained in the text. Your goal in the **Discover** step is to learn what the text *says* and not to find out what the text means. The **Discover** step is all about facts and content.

As noted, your powers of observation can be sharpened by applying "Helping Questions" (the five W's and one H questions) and "Helping Tools" to the selected text. Extra space has been left between the lines to provide room for highlighting, underlining, the circling of special words, etc.

But first we will begin with Helping Questions. Here are a few sample questions that will aid you in "*un*-covering" what God is saying in James 1:1-12. Again, we should note that the Greek word for "truth" is *alētheia* and literally means "no cover." So with the help of God and the illumination of the Spirit, the message of James will have "no cover" so that we might see it clearly.

As you address the Helping Questions below, write out your answers to each question. The very act of writing out the questions and answers will help you remember the data found in the text.

Sample Helping Questions

- Who are the "twelve tribes" mentioned in 1:1?

ANSWER

- What might be the difference between "trials" spoken of in 1:2 and "temptation" mentioned in 1:13? [Here you should know that the word for "trial" in the Greek (*peirasmos*) is the same word for "temptation." Also, this is the same word used by Jesus in the Lord's Prayer (Matt. 6:13). See also 1 Pet. 4:12].

ANSWER

- Why would James include a discussion on "wisdom" right after his treatment of "trials"?

ANSWER

Now it is your turn! In the space provided below, create your own questions and answer each of them. Remember to only create questions that you feel are important for understanding the text. Don't try to interpret the meaning of James at this point. This will come later. For now simply write out and answer questions that you feel *un*-cover what James is saying in this passage. There are no wrong questions here and you may find that you are not able to answer your own questions! The important thing is to purposefully think about what the text says. In any case, when you rejoin your class members for discussion, they will be able to benefit from what you have discovered and you will glean from their work as well.

So go on and create and answer some Helping Questions now.

MY HELPING QUESTIONS AND ANSWERS

Just in case your list of questions did not include the ones below, answer them now as well.

- Who is "James"? (Note: In answering this question, you might want to read and study Matt. 4:21, 10:2; Acts 1:13, 12:2, 17, 15:13; Gal. 1:19, 2:9-12; Jude 1:1).

ANSWER

- Why would a rich person take pride in the fact that his riches will soon pass away?

ANSWER

ANSWER CONTINUED

_____

_____

_____

_____

_____

Now is the time to reread all of the questions and answers you have worked through in the **Discover** step of IBS. Summarize your findings by asking yourself, "What are the facts that have arisen as a result of my work in this section?" Write out what you have _dis_-covered in the space provided.

MY FINDINGS

_____

_____

_____

_____

_____

_____

MY FINDINGS CONTINUED

 # DISCERN

Now that you have "pried out" some important facts from James 1:1-12, you are ready to go on to the **Discern** step of IBS. During the **Discover** step, you were intently focused on what the Scriptures *say*. Now in the **Discern** step you are concerned with what the Scriptures *mean*. If the operative word for the **Discover** step is *observation* then the operative word for the **Discern** step is *interpretation*.

In this step you will devise your own set of symbols and color coding to mark important features found in the text. Words that convey central aspects of the faith like *believe, salvation, sin, repentance,* and the like, should be marked. Instances of repetition, rhyming, comparisons, and contrasts should be noted as well. You may want to refer to the examples of commonly used symbols and marking systems that are used in *A Pentecostal Approach to Bible Study*. The important thing is that you use a system that makes sense to you. It should not only have meaning for this Bible study, but should also speak to you every time you study the Scriptures.

The **Discern** step is a critically important part of IBS. This is true because everything that you have been doing is to help you arrive at an informed interpretation of the Bible. Also, this is an intensely spiritual aspect of the interpretive process. There can be no true insight into the nature of God apart from the Spirit of God (1 Cor. 2:11). Now is the time to take a few moments and pray for God's guidance so that you can clearly hear His voice in the Scriptures.

PAUSE *for* PRAYER

The psalmist prayed, "Show me your ways, O Lord, teach me your paths" (Ps. 25:4). Only God can reveal God. We need to seek His revelation in all things, especially in understanding His Word. Just as the psalmist did, bow your head and pray that God reveal His ways as you study James. Ask Him now to teach you His paths.

As you reread James 1:1-12, you should have your colored pencils and highlighters ready. Now mark and comment on this passage as noted above. For example, throughout his entire epistle, James "paints" with words. That is, he likes to create "word pictures" to communicate his message. In this passage, James uses the word picture of a storm-tossed sea to describe a person who is filled with doubt (see 1:6). So you could use a wavy symbol highlighted in blue to represent doubt, instability, or a lack of trust.

Here are some tips that will help you **Discern** the meaning of this passage. These tips may also bring certain colors or symbols to mind that will help you choose symbols and markings for learning this passage.

- The word for "many kinds" in 1:2 is literally "many colored."

- The word for "testing" in 1:3 was used in the ancient world to test the value of gold coins. We still use the phrase "to test one's mettle" when speaking of the quality of one's character.

- The word for "generously" in 1:5 literally means "without folds." The picture is of a fine cloth that is spread out neatly so that nothing is hidden from sight.

- The word for "double-minded" in 1:8 is only found in the Epistle of James and means "two-souled." Today we might use the phrase "divided person" to translate this unique expression.

- James uses a special word for "grass stem" to communicate the image of a "wild flower" in 1:10. The same word is used in 1:11 and is translated "the plant." What James is saying is that the stem of the flower first dries up and then the petals fall off.

- The phrase "while he goes about his business" in 1:11 is literally "in his journeys," that is, "in all of his paths through life."

There is a lot more in this passage, so continue to write in symbols, highlight, and underline anything you feel will help you to understand God's message.

➡PULLING IT ALL TOGETHER⬅

Now that you have identified the important features of the passage, step back and observe the results of your work. Your use of Helping Questions and Helping Tools has no doubt led you to new insights in James 1:1-12. It is time to integrate all of these findings into an informed interpretation of the passage.

This part of IBS takes some patience. You will need to trace out each part of your marking system individually and jot down its significance. For example, if a certain color means "temptation" and that color appears in the center of the passage, you should note that the theme of temptation lies at the core of the section. This pattern of observation and notation should take place with each aspect of your marking system. As you **Discern** the significance of each part of your marking system, the "shape" of James' thought will appear. Thus after everything is taken together, the interpretation of the passage will gradually come together.

The following questions will help you draw together what has emerged thus far. Read each question, refer to the work you have done, and then jot down your response in the space provided.

- When a word is repeated in a passage, it usually points to an important concept for the author. Has James repeated any words in 1:1-12? If so, what is James telling us by means of these repetitions?

ANSWER

_____

_____

_____

_____

_____

_____

- James has set forth a number of contrasts in the passage. List these contrasts and write out what they might mean.

ANSWER

_____

_____

_____

_____

_____

_____

_____

- Have you noticed any "processes" or "progressions" in James thus far? What about the "trials → testing → perseverance" sequence? Write out your thoughts here and also note any other "progressions" found in this passage.

ANSWER

- Your marking system has no doubt revealed James' concern about the rich and the poor. Write out your thoughts here and compare what you have written with James 2:1-6 and 5:1-6.

ANSWER

ANSWER CONTINUED

_____

_____

_____

_____

_____

Now is literally your "moment of truth." Here you will draw together all that you have learned from the **Discover** step and join it to all of the meaning that has emerged from the **Discern** step. Here you will want to address the single, overarching question of "What is God saying in this passage?" In other words, in the light of your study thus far, what is the meaning of James 1:1-12? Write out your interpretation in the space provided below.

MY INTERPRETATION

_____

_____

_____

_____

_____

MY INTERPRETATION CONTINUED

DEVOTE

The important concepts in this step of the study are *commitment* and *obedience*. It is here that you, with the Lord's help, can be truly "inducted" or "drawn into" (remember the literal meaning of "induct"?) the Word. That is, now that you have a grasp on what the text means, you are now to ask, *What does this Scripture mean to me personally?* It is here that you should invite the Spirit to do an internal work in your heart.

The **Devote** step is arguably the most personal part of the whole study. This aspect of IBS surely needs to be "covered in prayer."

PAUSE *for* PRAYER

King David was no stranger to spiritual crises in his life. On one such occasion he prayed, "Cleanse me with hyssop, and I will be clean; wash me, and I will be whiter than snow" (Ps. 51:7). David knew that God alone was the answer to his spiritual needs. As you enter into the **Devote** section of IBS, can you pray this prayer with David? Can you plead with God that He affects real spiritual change in your life, the kind of change spoken forth in this lesson on James?

The following questions may help you to realize the kinds of change contained in James 1:1-12. Due to the deeply personal nature of these questions, there is no need to write down your responses here. However, you are strongly encouraged to record your thoughts in a spiritual journal or logbook. Journaling is a great way to express your commitment to God's voice as He speaks to you through His Word. There's just something about writing things down that strengthens one's resolve to follow through on one's commitments. In fact, as you work through James, your journal can become your personal covenant with the Bible. As a permanent record, your journal can call you back to obedience in the years to come.

So read the following questions prayerfully and ask, "What is God saying to me personally through this message of James?"

- Is God pleased with the way I have been responding to trials in my life (James 1:2)?
- Do I have enough "spiritual patience" to let God have His "perfect work" in my life (James 1:4 KJV)?
- In light of my spiritual journey thus far, where do I need God's wisdom most (James 1:5)?
- Am I a "divided person" before God? If so, what has caused me to doubt God and His Word?
- How do I really feel about the riches of this world?

Again, the Spirit may bring many additional questions to your mind. Be sensitive to the lessons James is teaching you. Be willing to undergo authentic change as you study through God's Word. Indeed, this part of IBS is a good time to experience one of the great graces of the Christian faith:

confession. The Greek word for "confession" is *homologeō,* which literally means "to say the same thing." As you work through James, and especially in the **Devote** step of IBS, be prepared "to say the same thing" as the Spirit. That is, be willing "to agree" with the Spirit concerning the shortcomings and sins in your life. And most importantly, be ready to allow the Spirit to do His perfect work in you as you study the Bible (see Heb. 13:21).

⳨ DISCIPLE

The ultimate goal of IBS is to change lives for God. It is here that all that has been learned must become "incarnate," not only in our lives, but also in the lives of others the Lord might place in our path. If the **Devote** step focused on the internal work of the Spirit, the **Disciple** step is concerned with the external manifestation of God in our lives. So the **Disciple** step of IBS challenges the serious student of the Bible to *real*-ize God's will on a day-to-day basis. The core idea here is, "What does the Scripture *require me to do?*" This means that the **Disciple** step is a call to *action*. It is the place in the study where you can make real plans to put what you have learned to work. The following are some personal commitments that can help you on your *path to discipleship.*

In light of what I have learned from James 1:1-12, *this week,* I commit to . . .

- Rejoice in the midst of trials, knowing in faith that God is working all things for my good (Rom. 8:28).

- Ask for divine wisdom when facing challenging times in my life.

- Take the path of faith and resist succumbing to doubt.

- Maintain a proper perspective on the material things of this world.

- Set my eyes on "the crown of life" rather than having my identity and future be determined by the values of this world.

As noted, not only are we to be discipled, but we are called to disciple others as well. That is, we are to use what we have learned in IBS to positively affect others for the kingdom of God. The **Disciple** step may be as simple as teaching others how to do inductive Bible study. On the other hand, the **Disciple** step may be a call to affect spiritual formation in the lives of others. In this case, you would bring the mandates of James 1:1-12 to bear on those whom God has placed in your care, always being dedicated to help them on their spiritual journey.

By now you have a feel for the "tone" of this great epistle. James is calling for authenticity in the life of the believer. He does not just want us to believe something; he wants us to act on what we believe. As he states, "Be ye doers of the word, and not hearers only, deceiving your own selves" (James 1:22 KJV). This will be the central theme of the next lesson.

A PENTECOSTAL APPROACH to BIBLE STUDY

LESSON TWO

James

1:13-27

REAL FAITH
IS NOT SHALLOW OR EMPTY

LESSON TWO
James 1:13-27
Real Faith Is Not Shallow or Empty

 ## KEY VERSE

Be ye doers of the word, and not hearers only, deceiving your own selves (James 1:22 KJV).

Introduction

By completing lesson one, you have already accomplished two major goals. First, you have learned how to do inductive Bible study. Second, you have gained insight into the heart and mind of James.

Lesson two will build upon these achievements. That is, since you already know the basics of IBS, there is no need to teach these interpretive principles again. Also, now that you have a feel for the way that James writes and for the issues that really matter to him, you will be better prepared to interpret the rest of the epistle.

You will soon discover that James 1:13-27 is a very rich portion of Scripture. It contains many themes that will be developed throughout the rest of the epistle. There is so much in this section that you might feel a bit overwhelmed at times as you study through this passage. However, the four steps of "**Discover . . . Discern . . . Devote . . . Disciple**" will serve as an interpretive roadmap to guide you on your *path to discipleship*. Also, the Helping Questions and Helping Tools of IBS will divide the study into manageable parts. With just a little patience, you will soon possess a much deeper understanding of God's Word in James.

Now it's time to start the next unit on our *path to discipleship*.

PAUSE *for* PRAYER

By now you know how essential prayer is for truly understanding the Bible. Proverbs 2:6 says, "For the Lord gives wisdom, and from his mouth come knowledge and understanding." Even before reading the text below, take a moment to pray for God's guidance. Pray that the Lord will enliven your heart so you can hear His voice as He speaks wisdom and understanding in the Epistle of James.

THE TEXT

James 1:13-27

[13]When tempted, no one should say, "God is tempting me." For God cannot be tempted by evil, nor does he tempt anyone; [14] but each one is tempted when, by his own evil desire, he is dragged away and

enticed. ¹⁵ Then, after desire has conceived, it gives birth to sin; and sin, when it is full-grown, gives

birth to death. ¹⁶ Don't be deceived, my dear brothers. ¹⁷ Every good and perfect gift is from above,

coming down from the Father of the heavenly lights, who does not change like shifting shadows. ¹⁸ He

chose to give us birth through the word of truth, that we might be a kind of firstfruits of all he created.

¹⁹ My dear brothers, take note of this: Everyone should be quick to listen, slow to speak and slow to

become angry, ²⁰ for man's anger does not bring about the righteous life that God desires. ²¹ Therefore,

get rid of all moral filth and the evil that is so prevalent and humbly accept the word planted in you,

which can save you. ²² Do not merely listen to the word, and so deceive yourselves. Do what it says.

²³ Anyone who listens to the word but does not do what it says is like a man who looks at his face in

a mirror ²⁴ and, after looking at himself, goes away and immediately forgets what he looks like. ²⁵ But the man who looks intently into the perfect law that gives freedom, and continues to do this, not

forgetting what he has heard, but doing it–he will be blessed in what he does. ²⁶ If anyone considers

himself religious and yet does not keep a tight rein on his tongue, he deceives himself and his religion

is worthless. ²⁷ Religion that God our Father accepts as pure and faultless is this: to look after orphans

and widows in their distress and to keep oneself from being polluted by the world.

ISCOVER

Remember that the main task here is to *dis*-cover what the text *says* and not to leap ahead and try to interpret what the text *means*. Here again you will employ the Helping Questions to pry out the important facts of James 1:13-27.

But first, carefully read the text to become thoroughly familiar with what James says here. As you read, be open to major features or ideas that leap off the page. Now reread the passage, looking even closer for details that move the story along in James 1:13-27.

Now that you have a good orientation to this section of Scripture, the use of Helping Questions will draw forth even more details of what James is saying in this important part of the Bible.

Sample Helping Questions

Here are a few Helping Questions that will assist you in your study. Write out your answer in the space provided.

- Why would some of James' recipients claim that God was tempting them?

  (In answering this question, you might want to note that the word for "tempt" in 1:13 is formed from the same word for "temptation/trial" as found in 1:2, 12).

ANSWER

- How would James' statement that God tempts no one relate to the Spirit leading Jesus into the wilderness to be tempted (Matt. 4:1-11; Mark 1:12-13)? What about Job 1:1-12?

ANSWER

- As noted, James likes progressions and sequences (see 1:10-11). What kind of progression or sequence do you see in 1:14-15?

ANSWER

- The words "dragged away" and "enticed" are used in the contexts of hunting and fishing. They describe attracting a fish with a lure or enticing an animal to enter a trap. How do these images inform your understanding of temptation?

ANSWER

- What examples from the Scriptures support James' claim that "sin gives birth to death?" List them here:

ANSWER

_____

_____

_____

_____

Now it is your turn to think creatively about the text. Make up some questions that you feel will clarify the vital elements contained in James 1:13-27. Write out your questions and then answer them in the space provided below.

MY HELPING QUESTIONS AND ANSWERS

_____

_____

_____

_____

_____

_____

MY HELPING QUESTIONS AND ANSWERS

If you haven't thought of these questions already, read and answer the following questions on

James.

- The phrase "Don't be deceived" in 1:16 is literally translated "Stop being deceived" rather than "Don't start to be deceived." How might this make a difference in understanding the message of James?

ANSWER

- What comes to mind when you read the phrase "Father of lights" in 1:17? What might this mean literally (see Gen. 1:1ff.)? What might the phrase mean symbolically (see John 1:1-14; 8:12)?

ANSWER

- The ancients were great stargazers, and James may be picking up on some of their imagery here. That is, the word for "variableness" (1:17 KJV) may echo the Greek word for "planet" which literally means "a wanderer" or "a waverer." What does 1:17 tell you about God's character?

ANSWER

- Also, the strange phrase "neither shadow of turning" (1:17 KJV) was used to refer to eclipses of the sun and moon. How does this relate to the image of the "Father of lights"?

ANSWER

At this point in your study, you should reread all of your helping questions and answers. Draw out all of the facts and content you have *dis*-covered through the **Discover** step of IBS. Summarize your findings in the space provided below. Remember that all of this information you have *un*-covered (remember the Greek word for "truth"!) will help you arrive at an informed interpretation of James 1:13-17. So take full advantage of your work, and write out everything you have learned about this section of the Bible.

MY FINDINGS

MY FINDINGS CONTINUED

_____

_____

_____

_____

_____

 # DISCERN

No doubt the Helping Questions have un-covered much of what James has said in 1:13-27. It's time to develop Helping Tools so you can understand what the text means. This is where the real work of interpretation takes place. Here again, we must seek the leading of the Holy Spirit in order to arrive at a correct interpretation of the Word.

PAUSE _for_ PRAYER

Give me understanding, and I will keep your law and obey it with all my heart (Ps. 119:34).

The psalmist reflects the two principal aims of IBS: _understanding_ and _obedience._ Therefore pray that God will help you *understand* the message of James so that you might *obey* the message of James. Indeed, understanding is the goal of the **Discern** step, while obedience is the goal of the **Devote** step.

Just as in lesson one, the **Discern** step uses a system of color coding, underlining, highlighting, and symbols to mark important themes, comparisons and contrasts, repetition, and so forth. Remember to be consistent in the use of these Helping Tools. If the color red signified the blood of Christ in lesson one, then red should signify the same in lesson two. So you might want to review the Helping Tools you used in lesson one and apply them here in lesson two as well. You will probably develop some new ones for this part of the study. That is to be expected, because each passage of Scripture makes unique contributions and so calls for its own color coding and marking system.

Here are some key areas that you might want to consider in James 1:13-27:

- Words that convey the idea of being tempted and temptation

- Elements of progression or development (Here you might want to use something like a series of arrows [→ → →] to indicate the idea of an ongoing process.)

- Images of birth and death

- Anything related to speaking or talking

- Ideas of being shallow or superficial

There are many more important elements contained in James 1:13-27, and it's your task to develop and apply an identifying system that will bring these aspects to light. So gather up all of your colored pencils and highlighters and mark up this passage.

➡PULLING IT ALL TOGETHER⬅

You now are on the verge of writing out your own interpretation of James 1:13-27. But first re-study what you have learned from your Helping Questions and relate all of this to your findings from the Helping Tools. The goal here is to coordinate all of the facts, patterns, and important concepts into one, cohesive interpretation. The following questions will help you accomplish this task.

- James uses a number of words for "tempt" or "temptation." Each use has its own special context. What is James telling us by using these words in their specific contexts?

ANSWER

- How does the "conception" of sin contrast with the "engrafting" of the Word?

ANSWER

- Note the image of a "good gift" that "comes down" from the Father (1:17). What does this remind you of in the Gospels (see Matt. 3:16; Luke 3:22)?

ANSWER

- James states, "For God cannot be tempted by evil, nor does he tempt anyone" (1:13). Yet Hebrews 4:15 states, " For we do not have a high priest who is unable to sympathize with our weaknesses, but we have one who has been tempted in every way, just as we are—yet was without sin." How can we reconcile these two verses? (In answering this question, you should keep in mind that the single Greek word translated by the phrase "cannot be tempted by evil" is an adjective describing the essential nature of God. That is, in God's essential nature He is "un-temptable.")

ANSWER

- What are some examples from Scripture that support James' claim that "sin brings forth death" (James 1:15)?

ANSWER

- In Romans 6:23 Paul teaches, "For the wages of sin is death, but the gift of God is eternal life through Christ Jesus our Lord." Does this reflect the theological principle set forth in James 1:15?

ANSWER

- James 1:18 states, "He chose to give us birth through the word of truth, that we might be a kind of firstfruits of all he created." What other writer in the New Testament speaks of being born of God? (See John 3:1-8; 1 John 2:29; 4:7; 5:1-4, 18).

ANSWER

- Look up other places in the Bible where it speaks of "firstfruits" (see Exod. 23:16-19; Exod. 34:22; Lev. 23:10; 1 Cor. 15:20-23; Rom. 8:23). How might these verses relate to James?

ANSWER

Now reread all that you have *dis*-covered by way of your Helping Questions and Helping Tools.

Draw all of these facts and insights together and write out your interpretation below.

MY INTERPRETATION

MY INTERPRETATION CONTINUED

_____

_____

_____

_____

_____

_____

_____

_____

_____

DEVOTE

You have reached the point in the lesson to "close the loop" so to speak. The aim of IBS is not only that "you get into" the Word, but that the Word *get into you.* Now that you know what the Scriptures mean, the critical question is, "What does the Scripture mean *to me*?" The significance of this question should be clear. New insight into the Bible only has value *if* it becomes part of your life. This is why the key verse of this lesson states, "Be ye doers of the word, and not hearers only, deceiving your own selves" (James 1:22 KJV).

The following questions might help you make the kinds of *commitments* and *obedience* that James 1:13-27 is addressing to your heart. But before entering into this next part of the lesson, it is good to seek God's direction in making this part of the Bible become real in your life.

PAUSE *for* PRAYER

In order to experience true spiritual growth in our lives, we must grant God permission to enter our hearts and make the necessary changes. The psalmist understood this when he prayed, "Search me, O God, and know my heart; test me and know my anxious thoughts" (Ps. 139:23). In light of what you have learned thus far in James, ask God to search your heart before engaging the questions listed next.

- Have I blamed God for deep hurts in my life? If so, what does this say about how I view God (James 1:13-18)?

- Does my speech reflect the character and heart of God (James 1:19)?

- Would Jesus have said some of the things I have said this day (James 1:26)?

- Are there "shallow" areas in my faith? Do I at times just hear the Word and quickly go on my way without understanding the deep claims God has placed upon my life (James 1:22-25)?

No doubt the Spirit has been speaking to you throughout your study of this powerful epistle. You may wish to write out God's "personal voice" to you in your journal or logbook. If you choose to keep such a journal, by the time you complete this study on James, you will have recorded an important spiritual journey in your life. This can serve as a key "reference work" for you as you continue to develop in the Lord.

✠ DISCIPLE

Here and there, the Gospels are punctuated with some "hard sayings" of Jesus. One of those is found in Mark 8:34. Here Jesus states, "Then he called the crowd to him along with his disciples and said: "If anyone would come after me, he must deny himself and take up his cross and follow me." At the time of Jesus, the words "take up one's cross" was the battle cry of a particularly militant group called the "Zealots." What they meant by this saying is that if you want to join our group, you will probably end up being crucified! Don't misunderstand. Jesus is not calling us to violence, but He is calling us to radical discipleship. He is calling us to engage in spiritual warfare for the Kingdom of God, regardless of the cost.

All of this means that the **Disciple** step of IBS is a radical call to action! The critical question is, "What does God want me *to do* in light of James 1:13-27?" James is calling us, with the help of God, to change. He is challenging us to a life of personal holiness. So in the light of the prophetic word of James, it is time to make a personal covenant with the Word. The following points will help you not only *hear* what James says but also to *do* what he says.

My personal covenant with James 1:13-27 *this week* is to:

- Stop blaming God for the temptations and failures that come into my life.

- Confess that every good and praiseworthy thing comes from the Father who is absolutely reliable and uncompromising in His character and values.

- Filter my speech through the mind of the Holy Spirit.

- Reject any shallow or superficial version of the faith.

- Take concrete and observable steps to actually help those who are less fortunate than me.

As you can see, the message of James is so relevant to the church today. James helps us answer the question, "How can I get the faith of my head to positively affect the faith of my heart, *and then* to go on to move my hands and feet to do the will of God?" The answer to this question forms a large part of what it means to go into all the world and make disciples (Matt. 28:19-20). That is, how can you use this **Disciple** step of IBS to influence others for God? What might this lesson mean to your circle of friends and family?

A PENTECOSTAL APPROACH

to

BIBLE STUDY

LESSON THREE

James

2:1-13

REAL FAITH
KEEPS THE PERFECT LAW OF LIBERTY

L E S S O N T H R E E

James 2:1-13

Real Faith Keeps the "Perfect Law of Liberty"

 ## KEY VERSE

Speak and act as those who are going to be judged by the law that gives freedom (James 2:12).

Introduction

You've accomplished a lot so far in your study of James! By using the **Discover . . . Discern . . . Devote . . . Disciple** method of IBS, you have established a "track record" in this type of Bible study. You are well on your way to making IBS your "go-to" method of studying God's word. Soon, if not already, the four D's of IBS will become second nature to you as you continue your journey through the Scriptures. Moreover, you have mastered the rich truths of James 1.

These include:

- The true nature of God

- The real source of temptation and its consequences

- The vast difference between just hearing the Word and actually doing what it says

Most importantly, you have allowed the Spirit to transform you through the renewing of your mind (Rom. 12:1-2). Lastly, you have committed to actualize the message of James in your life and seek to disciple others in the Word of God. Now the Spirit is poised to draw you (or be "induced"!) into the second chapter of James.

Before you begin though, prepare your heart through prayer so that you might receive all of the riches of God's Word in James 2:1-13.

PAUSE for PRAYER

As Moses was leading Israel through the wilderness, the Lord would often speak to him. The Scriptures state, "The Lord would speak to Moses face to face, as a man speaks with his friend" (Ex. 33:11). On one such occasion, Moses prayed, "If you are pleased with me, teach me your ways so I may know you and continue to find favor with you" (Ex. 33:13). It is interesting that this prayer occurred right before God gave the Law to Moses. Moses asked God to teach him His ways. In response, God revealed His Word to Moses. Right now, pray that God teach you His ways so you can be prepared to receive His Word.

THE TEXT

James 2:1-13

[1] My brothers and sisters, believers in our glorious Lord Jesus Christ must not show favoritism. [2] Suppose a man comes into your meeting wearing a gold ring and fine clothes, and a poor man in filthy old clothes also comes in. [3] If you show special attention to the man wearing fine clothes and say, "Here's a good seat for you," but say to the poor man, "You stand there" or "Sit on the floor by my feet," [4] have you not discriminated among yourselves and become judges with evil thoughts? [5] Listen, my dear brothers and sisters: Has not God chosen those who are poor in the eyes of the world to be rich in faith and to inherit the kingdom he promised those who love him? [6] But you have dishonored

the poor. Is it not the rich who are exploiting you? Are they not the ones who are dragging you into court? [7] Are they not the ones who are blaspheming the noble name of him to whom you belong? [8] If you really keep the royal law found in Scripture, "Love your neighbor as yourself," you are doing right.

[9] But if you show favoritism, you sin and are convicted by the law as lawbreakers. [10] For whoever keeps the whole law and yet stumbles at just one point is guilty of breaking all of it. [11] For he who said, "You shall not commit adultery," also said, "You shall not murder." If you do not commit adultery but do commit murder, you have become a lawbreaker. [12] Speak and act as those who are going to be judged by the law that gives freedom, [13] because judgment without mercy will be shown to anyone who has not been merciful. Mercy triumphs over judgment.

ISCOVER

Familiarize yourself with the text by carefully reading James 2:1-13. Take note of those main ideas that practically leap off the page as you work through the passage. Keep reading the passage until you are well oriented to the content of this section. Don't worry about what the text means; simply concentrate on what the text says. Actively sift through the passage in order to *un-cover* (do you still remember the Greek word for "truth"?) the facts that James has included here. In order to really "dig out" the message of James in chapter 2, you need to develop some Helping Questions. Remember, these are the five W's and the one H questions: Who? What? When? Where? Why? and How? Some sample questions are included below to help you along. Read through these questions and answer them to the best of your ability based on your careful reading of James 2:1-13.

Sample Helping Questions

- What type of favoritism might James be addressing in 2:1? (In answering this question reread 2:2-4.)

ANSWER

- What might James 2:2 tell us about the date and recipients of this important letter? (In answering this question you should know that the Greek word for "meeting" in the NIV and the word "assembly" in the KJV is literally "synagogue." That is, James does not use the word "church" in any place in his epistle; rather he uses the word "synagogue.")

ANSWER

- How might James 2:2-4 relate to James 1:9-11?

ANSWER

Now it is your turn to develop some Helping Questions. Recall that these questions should arise from your careful reading of the passage. This is why it is so important to read the text with a purpose. You are not just reading the Bible anymore. You are actively investigating each word and line to sift out the facts at hand.

Write out your questions, and answer each of them in the space provided below:

MY HELPING QUESTIONS AND ANSWERS

If you have not already included the questions that are listed below, read and answer these questions now.

- Why do you think James has included so much legal terminology, or language of the law court, in this section? (In answering this question, carefully review verses 2:4, 6, 11-13.)

ANSWER

- In using legal terminology, what is James telling us about the Final Judgment (see 2:12-13)?

ANSWER

- Why does James use the phrase "the royal law" in 2:8? (In answering this question, read Lev. 19:18; Matt. 19:19; 22:38-39; Rom. 13:9; Gal. 5:14).

ANSWER

As you can tell, well-crafted Helping Questions can really *dis*-cover the facts and content of any passage in the Bible. So it is time to revisit all of the questions and answers you have completed. In the space provided below, write out all of the important facts, phrases, and concepts you have learned by way of the **Discover** step of IBS.

MY FINDINGS

MY FINDINGS CONTINUED

_____

_____

_____

_____

_____

_____

_____

_____

_____

_____

_____

_____

 # DISCERN

Now that you have a good grasp on the content of James 2:1-13, you can proceed to explore what this passage means. That is, you are on the verge of rendering your own interpretation of this important passage of Scripture! Furthermore, by now you have become familiar with the process of the **Discern** step of IBS. You might want to take a moment and review the many Helping Tools you have developed in the previous lessons. This will help you remain consistent in how you apply your marking system and symbols. Also, as you read through the second chapter of James, you will be on the lookout for words, phrases, and themes that coincide with the marking system you have created. Be ready though to develop some totally new ways of noting important features in the Bible. In this way, by the time that you finish your study of James, you will have a whole treasury of Helping Tools that will stay with you for a lifetime.

But first, the special guidance of the Holy Spirit is needed to fully understand this important passage of Scripture. Take a moment to pray that God reveal the mystery of His Word (see Rom. 16:25).

PAUSE *for* PRAYER

The psalmist fully realized that the Lord must grant understanding if he was ever to obey God's Word. Thus he prayed, "Your hands made me and formed me; give me understanding to learn your commands" (Ps. 119:73). Pray now to your Creator, the One who made you, that He might grant you understanding. And as this lesson will bear out, the purpose of this understanding is so you might fully obey His commandments.

No doubt, you will want to reuse some of the Helping Tools that you have developed in previous lessons. Yet it is fun to think creatively and come up with new symbols and patterns for drawing forth the full meaning of James. For example, you might want to use the symbol of a balance scale, something like ⚖, to mark all words that speak of justice, judgment, and the like.

When applying your Helping Tools, some areas you will want to take note of are as follows:

- Words and phrases that reflect the injustice of favoritism

- Images of wealth and materialism

- Images of poverty and shame

- Words and phrases that speak of divine judgment

These suggestions are enough to get you started. Take your time and scrutinize the selected passage once again. Be ready to bracket, underline, or make brief comments in the margin so you might gain a deeper understanding of James 2:1-13. Once you are satisfied that you have tagged all of the important features of this section, proceed to "Pulling It All Together."

➡PULLING IT ALL TOGETHER⬅

Now you are ready to write out your interpretation of James 2:1-13. You should have a measure of confidence in this regard, because you have actively read the text through several times. Also, you have given considerable thought to the development of your Helping Questions and Helping Tools. The goal now is to integrate all of your findings into a single, well-informed interpretation. The following questions and comments will help you gather your thoughts in preparation for writing out your interpretation of this passage.

- James repeats the sequence of "rich . . . poor" several times in this passage. Write out the instances of "rich" or "poor" in James 2:1-13 and explain the significance of these words for James.

ANSWER

- Should the phrase "dragging you into court" (2:6) be taken literally or figuratively? Explain your answer.

ANSWER

- When James says, "slandering the noble name of him to whom you belong" (2:7), who might he be referring to?

ANSWER

- What does the statement, "Mercy triumphs over judgment!" (2:13) mean to you? Give examples to support your answer.

ANSWER

Now, in the light of all you have learned by way of your Helping Questions and Helping Tools, as well as your responses to the questions above, prayerfully write out your interpretation of James 2:1-13.

MY INTERPRETATION

DEVOTE

James is a straight talker. When writing out his epistle, he seems to have been guided by the words of Jesus, "Simply let your 'Yes' be 'Yes,' and your 'No,' 'No'; anything beyond this comes from the evil one" (Matt. 5:37). In fact, this is the very scripture he quotes in James 5:12! This direct, "no-holds-barred" kind of speech has a way of piercing us to the heart. In other words, the Spirit often uses James to "convict" our hearts. So in light of all you have learned from James 2:1-13, what is the Spirit saying to your heart right now? What areas of your life have been touched by the words of James in this section?

It is plain to see that the real work of the Word takes place in this **Devote** step of IBS. This is the place for spiritual formation to occur. This is also the place that sincere and fervent prayer is most needed. No one knew this more than the writer of this epistle. James states, "The prayer of a righteous man is powerful and effective" (James 5:16).

PAUSE for PRAYER

In Luke 10:22, Jesus said, "All things have been committed to me by my Father. No one knows who the Son is except the Father, and no one knows who the Father is except the Son and those to whom the Son chooses to reveal him." From this scripture, we see that no one can "storm the gates of heaven," so to speak, and carry away a knowledge of God (see Prov. 30:2-4). True knowledge of God and authentic relationship to Him is a gift; it is a revelation. As you prepare to be "induced" or "drawn into" the power of this message from James, pray that the Son reveal the heart of the Father and, most importantly, that you fully respond to His voice in James.

The following questions and comments may help you invite God's change in your life. Indeed, the word for "repent" in Greek is metanoeō, which literally means, "to change the mind." So one truly repents when he or she "changes the mind" toward God, toward the self and toward others. As you commit to this Devote step, prayerfully ask yourself, "What does James want me to change my mind about?" This would be a good time to write in your journal or logbook. Also, you can return to what you have written and use these thoughts to guide your devotions throughout the coming week.

- Do you pay more respect to a wealthy person than to a poor person? If so, what does this say about how you value others?

- Do you really believe that the meek (or poor?) will inherit the earth (Matt. 5:5)?

- Have I treated my neighbor (that is, persons close to me) as I would like them to treat me (James 2:8)?

- Do I fully acknowledge that, in one way or another, I am a "lawbreaker" (James 2:11)?

As you go through this week, allow the challenges of James 2:1-13 to speak to your heart. Prayerfully meditate on the lessons of this section and seek to fully embrace its teachings.

✞ DISCIPLE

By nature, the **Devote** step of IBS is very contemplative and introspective. On the other hand, the challenge of the **Disciple** step is to actualize God's Word in your daily life. James would have rejoiced in this aspect of IBS! The Epistle of James is all about putting our faith into practice. So in this part of the study, you should ask yourself, "What can I *do* to make the words of James real in my life?" For example, for the pure sake of spiritual *discipline* (which is the root word for "*disciple*") you might commit to publicly affirming the poor (James 2:1-7). Go out of your way to make a less fortunate person feel special in the midst of the community of faith. Also, you might seek concrete ways to "love your neighbor as yourself" (James 2:8). This might involve hospital visitation or writing a letter of encouragement to someone in need. Finally, someone you know needs to experience the mercy of God (James 2:12-13). Throughout this week, be on the lookout for those who might be spiritually exhausted and thus need the merciful presence of a caring friend.

Yet these decisive moments in discipleship are not to end with you. You are also to go out and make disciples. Throughout this week, you should ask yourself, "In what ways can I expand the impact that James has had on my life?" Could you give a devotional, either formal or informal, on what you have learned in James? Finally, with regard to James 2:1-13, can you be an instrument of change for God in your circle of family and friends? This is discipleship in action! Make every effort to "induct" others into the world-changing teachings of James!

A PENTECOSTAL APPROACH *to* BIBLE STUDY

LESSON FOUR

James

2:14-26

REAL FAITH
IS NEVER INVISIBLE

LESSON FOUR

James 2:14-26

Real Faith Is Never Invisible

 ## KEY VERSE

As the body without the spirit is dead, so faith without deeds is dead (James 2:26).

Introduction

You are well on your way to becoming a master of inductive Bible study. These skills, together with your understanding of the mind of James, will unlock the hidden truths found in James 2:14-26. In this section, James sounds more like an Old Testament prophet than an early Christian preacher. His language is confrontational. He even includes elements of irony and sarcasm. All of this is to jolt his readers out of a spiritual slumber that threatens to slip into death. He incessantly drives home the single point: a "faith" that has nothing to show for it is really no faith at all. Such a faith is hollow, so thin and weak as to be invisible. A faith that refuses to become a living source of healing, redemption, and benevolence has nothing to do with the authentic faith-vision of the people of God. So brace yourself for the unflinching voice of the apostle James!

PAUSE for PRAYER

If ever there was a time to pray over a lesson, this is the time. In this passage, James sounds like the prophet Jeremiah when he states, "But if I say, 'I will not mention him or speak any more in his name,' his word is in my heart like a fire, a fire shut up in my bones. I am weary of holding it in; indeed, I cannot" (Jer. 20:9). James cannot hold in the Word of God. If we take his message seriously, and that is the whole goal of IBS, then his words burn deep in our hearts. Yet with the help of the Holy Spirit, the Epistle of James can be a purifying fire in our lives (Matt. 3:11) rather than a message of destruction (James 3:5-6). So as you prepare to enter into this next section of James, receive the prayer that Jesus prayed for His disciples: "Sanctify them by the truth; your word is truth" (John 17:17). Indeed the Greek word for "sanctify" is *hagiazō* and literally means "to set apart as sacred unto God." Therefore, as you work through this important passage, pray that God "set you apart" for His sacred work.

THE TEXT

James 2:14-26

14 What does it profit, my brethren, if someone says he has faith but does not have works? Can faith save him? 15 If a brother or sister is naked and destitute of daily food, 16 and one of you says to them, "Depart in peace, be warmed and filled," but you do not give them the things which are needed for the body, what does it profit? 17 Thus also faith by itself, if it does not have works, is dead. 18 But someone will say, "You have faith, and I have works." Show me your faith without your works, and I will show you my faith by my works. 19 You believe that there is one God. You do well. Even the demons believe—and tremble! 20 But do you want to know, O foolish man, that faith without works is dead? 21 Was not Abraham our father justified by works when he offered Isaac his son on the altar? 22 Do you see that

faith was working together with his works, and by works faith was made perfect? [23] And the Scripture

was fulfilled which says, "Abraham believed God, and it was accounted to him for righteousness." And

he was called the friend of God. [24] You see then that a man is justified by works, and not by faith only.

[25] Likewise, was not Rahab the harlot also justified by works when she received the messengers and sent

them out another way? [26] For as the body without the spirit is dead, so faith without works is dead also.

DISCOVER

The real "spade work" of the lesson occurs in the **Discover** step of IBS. You will want to carefully

read through James 2:14-26 several times so that you can "dig out" the important facts of the text. You

need to apply all of your investigative powers so that you might sift out all that James has to offer in

this special passage of Scripture. Just as an archaeologist uses a variety of tools to "un-cover" precious

artifacts of biblical history, you must also employ an array of Helping Questions to bring important features to light in James. This is why you need to resist the temptation to jump right in and randomly pick an item or two from the passage. You must first become thoroughly oriented to the "cite" so that you don't overlook a key find, or worse yet, accidentally destroy something important. So, patiently examine the passage, layer by layer, until you are at last drawn into the heart of its meaning.

As usual, some sample Helping Questions are provided to get you going in the right direction. Answer each question to the best of your ability, all the while keeping in mind that you will develop your own Helping Questions later on.

Sample Helping Questions

- What is the expected answer to James' question in 2:14?

ANSWER

JAMES IS EXPECTING A NO

- In the context of our present society and culture, how would you describe the persons set forth in 2:15?

ANSWER

- What kind of attitude is James describing in 2:16?

ANSWER

At this point, it is your turn to create some Helping Questions. Remember that these questions are based on your thorough reading of James 2:14-26. Craft your questions carefully so they *dis*-cover the controlling ideas and facts in the passage. All of this is contributing to your ability to give a solid interpretation of the Bible.

Write out your questions and answers in the space provided.

MY HELPING QUESTIONS AND ANSWERS

Here are some additional questions that will help you master the content of James 2:14-26.

- How could one evidence his or her faith without deeds or any observable action (2:18)?

ANSWER

- What kind of "faith" do the demons have (2:19)?

ANSWER   THEY BELIVE THERE IS ONE GOD

- Where in the Bible does it say that Abraham was called God's friend (2:23)?

ANSWER   GOD
II CHRONICALY 20:7

By carefully reading through the passage several times and by answering all of the Helping Questions, you have identified many important facts and features of James 2:14-26. In order to further clarify what you have found, reread all of the Helping Questions and answers and summarize the results in the space provided.

MY FINDINGS

FAITH & WORKS GO TOGETHER.

NOT THAT FAITH NEEDS
WORKS TO EXIST BUT

FAITH NEEDS WORK TO

SHOW IT IS ALIVE AND WELL

DISCERN

James 2:14-26 poses special challenges for the **Discern** step of IBS. This is true because James includes many hard sayings in this passage. He speaks about demons believing, Abraham being justified by works, and even commends a Gentile harlot named Rahab. For all of these reasons, the student must be wise and thorough in his or her use of the Helping Tools. Indeed, this section represents one of the more perilous portions of James. It would be easy to go off on the wrong track and arrive at a flawed interpretation. Thus, it would be wise to seek the special guidance of the Spirit in searching out the sense of this passage.

PAUSE *for* PRAYER

In reference to Jesus Christ, Hebrews 10:7 states, "Then I said, 'Here I am—it is written about me in the scroll—I have come to do your will, O God.'" What a clear and forceful expression of obedience! Jesus did not come to think about the will of God or even to just talk about the will of God. On the contrary, the Lord came *to do* the will of God. And this is the point of James 2:14-26. True faith does the will of God. Pray now that God grant you the power to have an "action-driven" faith!

Make sure to devise a way to contrast James' use of "faith" with the way he uses "works" or "deeds." Also, note the cooperation of faith with works in this section. You might want to devise a symbol of cooperation like this ⟋⟍ to indicate that faith must be "linked to" works. Also the term "dead" is often repeated in this passage. You might want to use something like a bold "X" or a dead fish (⟩⫘⟩) to mark all of the references to death in 2:14-26.

These last two symbols evidence a principle of learning that you probably already discovered. Often the more unusual a symbol is, the easier it will be to remember what it stands for. That's why it is important for you to develop your own symbols. The ones you create personally will stay with you longer and be more meaningful than simply borrowing a marking system from someone else. All of this is designed to fix the meaning of the Scriptures firmly in your mind so that you can *disciple* others in the Lord.

The following are some unique aspects found in James 2:14-26. These will help you to develop your Helping Tools for this important passage.

- The word for "deeds" or "works" found in 2:14, 17-18, 20-22, 24-26 is built on the Greek root for "energy." You can see how *active*, *forceful*, and *strong* James' word for "works" is!

- The word for "show" in 2:19 literally means, "to point out with the finger." James can "point to" observable actions that evidence his faith in God.

- Some form of "complete," "mature," or "perfect" is used in 1:4, 15, 25; 2:8 and 2:22. What types of "completion" or "maturity" is James speaking of in these verses?

- Read and study the story about Abraham offering up Isaac in Genesis 22:1-19. Now allow this account to inform your study of James 2:21-24.

➡PULLING IT ALL TOGETHER⬅

Continue to mark, highlight, and comment on this section of Scripture until you feel that you have identified all of the key ideas, words, and patterns of the passage.

It is time to harvest all of the fruit of your labor (see 2 Tim. 2:6)! You can now bring together all of the facts *dis*-covered by your Helping Questions and all of the key elements revealed by your Helping Tools and blend them together into a single, flowing interpretation of James 2:14-26. The following points will serve as guidelines to collect your thoughts on this important passage.

- James uses a number of rhetorical questions throughout this passage. A rhetorical question is one that expects a certain answer. For example, when the waiter at a restaurant asks, "How may I help you today?" you would not answer, "Change the oil in my car." No! The expected answer to the waiter's rhetorical question is to recite part of the printed menu. In a similar way, James has posed a number of questions to his recipients of which he expects a particular answer. What kinds of answers does James expect in the questions found in 2:14, 16, 20-21 and 25? Write out your responses in the space provided below.

ANSWER

ANSWER CONTINUED

- James implies that Abraham was justified by works (see 2:21-22). But the apostle Paul adamantly denies that a person is justified by works and also uses Abraham as an example of a person who was justified by faith alone, and not by works (see Rom. 4:1-5). How can you reconcile the views of James and Paul here?

ANSWER *WORK, DO NOT MAKE FAITH SAVING BUT SHOW IT IS TRUE TO OUTSIDERS*

- The word that James uses for "tremble" (KJV), or "shudder" with fear in 2:19 is built on the idea of frizzy hair standing on end. How does this special word influence your interpretation?

ANSWER *WE ARE TO WORK WITH OUR FAITH TO IT ON THE OUTSIDE & WORK*

ANSWER CONTINUED

Now you are ready to gather up all that has been revealed to you as a result of your careful work with James. Use all of this insight to write out your interpretation on the space provided.

MY INTERPRETATION

DEVO✝E

It would be difficult to walk away from James 2:14-26 without sensing the need for change. The inherent expectation of the Scriptures is that our faith in God will make a real difference in how we live in the world. As the apostle John says, "If anyone has material possessions and sees his brother in need but has no pity on him, how can the love of God be in him?" (1 John 3:17). It is clear that for James, real faith involves an essential transformation of everything that we say and do. This is what the **Devote** step is all about—allowing the Spirit to actualize God's Word in our lives. Yet this requires a kind of spiritual pursuit that only prayer can affect. As Jesus said, "Blessed are those who hunger and thirst for righteousness, for they will be filled" (Matt. 5:6). Do you have that kind of hunger for an authentic faith—the kind of faith that James speaks of in this lesson?

PAUSE *for* PRAYER

In one of the most intriguing books of the Bible, Job reflects upon his life in God.

Whoever heard me spoke well of me, and those who saw me commended me, because I rescued the poor who cried for help, and the fatherless who had none to assist him. The man who was dying blessed me; I made the widow's heart sing. I put on righteousness as my clothing; justice was my robe and my turban. I was eyes to the blind and feet to the lame. I was a father to the needy; I took up the case of the stranger (Job 29:11-16).

Examine his statement closely. Why did he have such a sterling reputation among the people? The answer is because people *observed* his care for the poor, the fatherless, the infirmed, and the widow. In the same way, James would have us pray that we see with God's eyes, speak with God's voice, and help with God's hands. Furthermore, these real expressions of our faith must be *observable*.

The following remarks are designed to provide structure for your prayers. Indeed, this portion of James makes for a good "pray and write" session. So take out your journal, read one of the items below, pray about it, and then write your reflections down.

- If you never spoke a word again, could perfect strangers tell that you are a Christian (James 2:18)?

- Have you ever observed a real need and for some reason or other, simply walked away (James 2:15-16)? How did that make you feel? Why do you think that is so?

- With regard to faith and works, James seems to be calling for a perfect balance between the two. Percentagewise for James, an ounce of faith produces an ounce of good deeds, so to speak. How about the ratio of faith to works in your life? Is it 50/50? 75/25? 90/10? As an experiment, try to determine how much of what you believe actually makes life better for those around you. Write out a figure. Now pray about that figure and seek to hear God's voice in this regard.

⟨✝⟩DISCIPLE

James demands a godly life that is enlivened by an authentic faith. As you have probably noted already, much of what he says sounds like the Sermon on the Mount (Matt. 5:1-48). Like Jesus, his words are beautiful and terrifying altogether! If at times you don't feel a bit overwhelmed by James, then you are not reading him closely enough. But with God, all things are possible (Matt 19:26). The following commitments will help you build an action-filled faith—the kind of faith that James would be proud of.

This week I commit to . . .

- seek out at least one person in need and to take specific action to meet that need.
- put "shoe leather" to my prayers. That is, if I feel burdened enough to pray about something, I will be burdened enough to do something about it.

With regard to making disciples, many sincere believers want to help, but they don't know how. Perhaps you could identify a community need and organize a relief effort to meet that need. There are so many things we can do to actualize our faith. And when we do, we will fulfill the words of Jesus when He said, "In the same way, let your light shine before men, that they may see your good deeds and praise your Father in heaven" (Matt 5:16). To that, James would say, "Amen!"

A PENTECOSTAL APPROACH
to
BIBLE STUDY

LESSON FIVE

James

3:1-9

REAL FAITH
SPEAKS TRUE

L E S S O N   F I V E

James 3:1-9

Real Faith Speaks True

 ## KEY VERSE

The tongue also is a fire, a world of evil among the parts of the body. It corrupts the whole person, sets the whole course of his life on fire, and is itself set on fire by hell (James 3:6).

Introduction

You have come a long way on your journey through James. You are by now very familiar with the tone of this epistle. James comes across more like a preacher than a teacher. He sounds much more like a prophet than a pastor. Yet he's good medicine for the soul! James, like a caring physician, has our best interest in mind, even though he must take extreme measures at times. In our last lesson on 2:14-26, James exposed how worthless faith can be if it has no real expression in life. In that lesson, he challenged his readers to take faith-filled action so that they could make a real difference in the lives of hurting people. In 3:1-9, James is not so much concerned about what *we do* as he is about what *we say*. So in the previous lesson, James demanded right *action*; in this lesson, James demands right *speech*.

Let it be emphasized once again. What James sets forth in 3:1-9 can literally transform our relationship to God and how we relate to those about us. This is not an overstatement! If we allow the grace of God to apply this lesson to our hearts, and if we seek the help of the Holy Spirit to obey, our lives will never be the same again after studying this portion.

This kind of help can only come by way of prayer. Take a moment to read through the passage for this lesson and then pray that God will help you to not only *understand* His Word but also to *do* His Word.

PAUSE *for* PRAYER

In Isaiah 59:21, the Lord says: "As for me, this is my covenant with them . . . My Spirit, who is on you, and my words that I have put in your mouth will not depart from your mouth, or from the mouths of your children, or from the mouths of their descendants from this time on and forever." What a wonderful promise from the Lord! Not only is the Spirit promised to us and our offspring (Acts 2:17-18; Joel 2:28), but God will put His words into our mouth . . . forever. The close association of the Spirit and godly speech is no accident. In order to truly speak for another, one must know the heart of another. And this is James' point in 3:1-9. The words we speak should come from the heart of God. Therefore as you work through this session, pray for an extraordinary presence of the Spirit—the kind of presence that will put the very words of God in your mouth.

 # THE TEXT

James 3:1-9

¹Not many of you should presume to be teachers, my brothers, because you know that we who teach

will be judged more strictly. ² We all stumble in many ways. If anyone is never at fault in what he says,

he is a perfect man, able to keep his whole body in check. ³ When we put bits into the mouths of horses

to make them obey us, we can turn the whole animal. ⁴ Or take ships as an example. Although they

are so large and are driven by strong winds, they are steered by a very small rudder wherever the pilot

wants to go. ⁵ Likewise the tongue is a small part of the body, but it makes great boasts. Consider what a great forest is set on fire by a small spark. [6] The tongue also is a fire, a world of evil among the parts of the body. It corrupts the whole person, sets the whole course of his life on fire, and is itself set on fire by hell. [7] All kinds of animals, birds, reptiles and creatures of the sea are being tamed and have been tamed by man, [8] but no man can tame the tongue. It is a restless evil, full of deadly poison. [9] With the tongue we praise our Lord and Father, and with it we curse men, who have been made in God's likeness.

DISCOVER

Since James addresses a single topic in this section—that is, the topic of wayward speech—the challenge of the **Discover** step is made somewhat easier. Clearly, the present task is to develop those Helping Questions that "lift out" all facts that relate to sinful speech in James 3:1-9. So as in the other lessons, carefully read the passage, and be on the alert for important words and controlling ideas. The following questions will help you find those words and ideas that are essential to the content of James 3:1-9.

Sample Helping Questions

- Whom is James specifically addressing in 3:1?

Aɴsᴡᴇʀ

- Where else can you find the word *judgment* in James? (Note: In answering this question, carefully reread James 2:1-3:1.)

Aɴsᴡᴇʀ

5 LESSON FIVE

- How would you describe the general principle that James sets forth in 3:3-5?

ANSWER

There is a lot more content to be uncovered in 3:1-9. You need to develop your own Helping Questions to pry out the facts of this demanding portion of the Bible. The harder you work on creating good Helping Questions, the more accurate your final interpretation will be. So take some time to write out questions and include your answers below.

MY HELPING QUESTIONS AND ANSWERS

MY HELPING QUESTIONS AND ANSWERS CONTINUED

Here are a couple more questions that may help you grasp the content of this section:

- How would you describe the general principle found in James 3:11-12?

ANSWER

- Where do you think James might have obtained the word-picture in 3:7?

ANSWER

Your careful reading of the text, as well as creating and answering Helping Questions, have certainly granted you considerable insight into the content of James 3:1-9. You should reread all that you have written thus far and summarize your findings below. The very act of writing your responses down will help you organize your thoughts so you can render a good interpretation later on. So think through your work thus far and summarize what you have learned in the space provided.

My Findings

DISCERN

James 3:1-9 contains some of the most vivid word-pictures in the New Testament. This makes for a lot of fun when creating Helping Tools for this section. For example, you will want to bring over the ⚖ symbol again to mark aspects concerning judgment and justice. Or you might use something like 🛑 to indicate "control" over the way we speak to others. The many contrasts in this section can be indicated by the ≠ sign. There are many possibilities for this very picturesque section of James. Yet always keep the goal in sight. Your marking symbols and highlighting are to help bring out the sense of the Bible. In the **Discern** step, you are to focus on what the Scriptures mean. So everything you do in this **Discern** step is to move you in the direction of that goal.

In addition to being one of the most colorful sections of the Bible, James 3:1-9 is one of the most confrontational as well. Yet as noted at the start of this lesson, James has only our welfare in mind. So before you begin marking and commenting on this important part of the Bible, stop and seek God's guidance in your work. This is what tailors IBS to your individual life context and makes this kind of study so powerful. So pray for the Spirit's leading as you are drawn deep into the heart of James.

PAUSE *for* PRAYER

"May the words of my mouth and the meditation of my heart be pleasing in your sight, O Lord, my Rock and my Redeemer" (Ps. 19:14). With this prayer, the psalmist gets to the heart of James' teaching in 3:1-9. He understood that the words we speak originate in the musings of our heart. In the same way, Jesus taught that it is not what goes into a person that leads to spiritual defilement, but what comes out of a person by way of what he or she says—this is what undermines our spirit (Mark 7:18-22). Pray that God use this lesson on James to accomplish two things in your life. First, pray that James' message fundamentally alters the way you think and feel in your heart. Second, pray that as a result of God's sanctifying work in your heart there will be corresponding change in the way you speak. This is what James is after in this section.

The following comments are designed to address some major features of this special passage. They are intended to help you render a good interpretation of James 3:1-9. Also they may inspire you to create some unique symbols or marking devices that will help you remember and understand this vital message of James.

- There are many "controlling" elements in this passage (for example, "guiding," "steering," and "taming"). Be sure to note all of these instances and seek to *discern* their full meaning.
- Contrast the strong winds in 3:4 with the wind of 1:6.
- Note the "small → large" pattern of this passage and relate it to the "tongue → body" image.

Now continue to highlight and mark important ideas, phrases and special features of James. Remember that you have enough data by way of the Helping Questions to start discerning the meaning of James 3:1-9. Make an effort to use all of your previous symbols and markings. With each lesson you are adding to your "toolbox" of interpretive helps. All this means that by the grace of God you are becoming more skilled in interpreting the Bible.

➡PULLING IT ALL TOGETHER⬅

Now is the time to draw upon all of the rich insight you have gained from the use of your Helping Questions and Helping Tools. Reread all of your questions and answers, and study closely all of the highlighting, underlining, color-coding, etc., that you employed during the **Discern** step of IBS. Look for connections and emphases. Draw out the sense of each fact and word-picture you have observed thus far and begin to organize your thoughts on what God is saying in James 3:1-9. The following comments will provide you a framework for crafting an interpretation of this challenging portion of Scripture.

- Look up other places where "teachers" is mentioned in the New Testament. Why might James have a special concern for teachers in 3:1? Write your response in the space provided.

ANSWER

- The same Greek word for "stumble" (or "offend" KVJ) used in 3:2 is also used in 2:10. Compare these two uses and explain how they might relate to one another.

ANSWER

- Why does James bring up the person of God in 3:9 and then immediately mention the "image of God" in humans? How might this serve his purpose of emphasizing the destructiveness of human speech?

ANSWER

- In 3:6, James uses the phrase "the whole course of his [a person's] life" or "the course of nature" (KJV). In the Greek, the phrase literally means "the wheel of creation." What do you think James means by this unique phrase? What are some contemporary expressions that might convey what James is saying here?

ANSWER

By this point, you have gathered enough data and discerned enough meaning in the text that you are ready to write out a sound interpretation for all of James 3:1-9. Coordinate all of the sense that you have been able to derive from your work and write out a complete interpretation.

MY INTERPRETATION

MY INTERPRETATION CONTINUED

_____

_____

_____

_____

_____

_____

DEVOTE

It is interesting to note that James emphasizes we have been created in the image of God (see Gen 1:26-27). Also, our first introduction to God in the Bible lets us know that God is a speaking God (Gen 1:3). We too, being created in God's likeness, are able to speak. So there is something "divine" about human speech. Yet because of the Fall (see Gen 3:1-24), James says there is something devilish about human speech as well. Indeed, it would be difficult to read the text of this lesson without sensing the conviction of the Holy Spirit! This is true because, as James has said, "we all stumble in many ways" (James 3:2) and then he goes on to vividly portray sins of speech. Just how we communicate with one another merits a continual state of prayer.

PAUSE *for* PRAYER

As you well know, the **Devote** step is all about change! It is here that the Spirit challenges us to "own" the interpretation we've worked so hard to produce. And with regard to how we speak, we need the constant mentoring of the Spirit. There is no shame in this, for even the prophet Isaiah needed special grace to speak on behalf of God. He lamented, "Woe to me! . . . I am ruined! For I am a man of unclean lips, and I live among a people of unclean lips, and my eyes have seen the King, the Lord Almighty" (Isa. 6:5). But then a seraph (an angelic heavenly being; see Isa 6:2, 6) took a burning ember from the altar of God and touched Isaiah's lips. In this way Isaiah's speech was cleansed by divine fire. He became a fit vessel to speak for God (Isa 6:7). Indeed, the word catharsis is directly taken from the Greek word *katharizō* which means "to cleanse" (see James 4:8; Acts 15:9; 1 John 1:7). Pray that the fire of the Holy Spirit continually cleanse your speech so that you can be a pure voice for Him (see Matt. 3:11; Luke 3:16).

The following remarks are offered to help you welcome James' challenges into your life. Prayerfully read each one and allow God to speak to the areas of your life that are in need of change. James' challenge is deeply personal. After all, what could be more personal than the verbal expression of our inmost thoughts? Herein lays the strength of keeping a journal or logbook. You are able to record how you respond to James at this time. The point here is that the work of God in our lives does not always happen all at once. It often takes time. So as the Lord continues to work in your life, you can revisit your journal and see the progress you have made.

- Even if you don't view yourself as a teacher (James 3:1), the Great Commission requires every Christian to "teach" as we go out and make disciples (Matt. 28:19-20). This means that the lessons contained in James 3:1-9 are binding upon every true believer.

- On a scale of 1-10, with 10 representing complete control, in your opinion how much control do you have over what you say?

- Of all the images that James uses to describe uncontrolled speaking, which one describes you best?

- If no one can tame the tongue (James 3:8), then who can tame it?

Although we have all been created in God's image, even as James has said in 3:9, each of us is unique in our personalities and experience. This means that God may be speaking to you very differently than what has been outlined above. In any case, though, God wants us all to be conformed into the image of His Son (Rom. 8:29). This means with regard to what we say to others, we are not to be conformed to this world, but rather *transformed* through the renewing of our minds (Rom. 12:2). This is what the **Devote** step of IBS is all about. And this too is what James 3:1-9 is all about—the transformation of our words into the words of Jesus.

✝⟨⟩DISCIPLE

James is not satisfied with the believer entertaining good thoughts. He is all about good action. This is the heart of discipleship! We are to welcome, affirm, and empower God's redeeming action in our lives. Perhaps the most public and influential way that this happens is through what we say. A lifetime of work can be undermined by a single, careless word. This **Disciple** step is designed to keep this from happening in your life.

The following are some practical commitments that can help make your everyday speech more pleasing to God.

This week I commit to . . .

- "Be quick to listen, slow to speak and slow to become angry" (James 1:19)

- Filter my comments through the mind of Christ (Rom. 12:2)

- Only say words that reflect Philippians 4:8

- Say a word of encouragement to at least one person in need of praise (Rom. 14:19)

- Continually ask myself, "Is what I am about to say making things better or worse?" If the latter, then I refuse to say it (see Titus 2:7-8).

James' message in 3:1-9 poses some real challenges with regard to discipling others. This is true because the way we communicate is so closely linked to our personal identity. So it can be a delicate matter to mentor others on how they speak. When we try to help people in what they say, we could easily be misunderstood. It may be that your area of influence in this aspect of discipleship consists of only one or two persons. Even so, you will need a healthy dose of the spiritual medicine offered up by James in the next lesson—that is, you will need the wisdom of God.

A PENTECOSTAL APPROACH
to
BIBLE STUDY

LESSON SIX

James

3:10-18

REAL FAITH
SPEAKS WISDOM

LESSON SIX
James 3:10-18
Real Faith Speaks Wisdom

 ## KEY VERSE

Who is wise and understanding among you? Let him show it by his good life, by deeds done in the humility that comes from wisdom (James 3:13).

Introduction

Is there a difference between wisdom and knowledge? Or one could ask, is there a distinction between "the facts at hand" and decisions that are made on the basis of one's character and values? Are there different kinds of wisdom? Is being "streetwise" or "worldly-wise" the same thing as acting in good judgment? If there are indeed different kinds of wisdom, what kind of wisdom does God affirm? What kind does He reject?

These are the types of questions James seeks to resolve in 3:10-18. In a way, he is really emphasizing the **Discern** step of IBS in this section. He is calling on his readers *to interpret* what is the true wisdom from God and what is the false wisdom of the world.

121

This kind of interpretation is especially hard for us who live in a Western culture. Whether we realize it or not, we in America have inherited a mind-set that welcomes facts, data, and figures. We value the kind of knowledge that gets the job done. We often harbor a "whatever-works" mentality. People who are skilled at "working the system" and "making it happen" we tend to label "smart" and "sharp." These kinds of people know how to "get ahead." On the other hand, those who have far different bases for decision making, well . . . we have other names for them. The critical issue here, especially for James, is what should be the mind-set, or the "standard operating procedure" for the Christian. Should the believer always opt for the ways of the Kingdom or are there occasions when, if you are going to beat the world you have to be the world? It is these kinds of distinctions, the difference between the wisdom of God and the wisdom of the world, that James would have us pray about!

PAUSE *for* PRAYER

"Blessed is the man who finds wisdom, the man who gains understanding, for she is more profitable than silver and yields better returns than gold" (Prov. 3:13-14). With regard to the kinds of questions posed above, the writer of Proverbs has already given his answer. There is a wisdom that is more valuable than anything this world can offer. This wisdom cares nothing about investment strategies and stock options. This wisdom does not obsess about how to climb the corporate ladder.

In fact, its point of reference has nothing to do with this world. On the contrary, this wisdom finds its home in the heart of God. This is the kind of wisdom that James is committed to.

Take a moment and pray that God will give you the ability to *discern*, as James says, "the wisdom that comes from heaven" (James 3:17).

 # THE TEXT

James 3:10-18 (NKJV)

[10] Out of the same mouth proceed blessing and cursing. My brethren, these things ought not to be so.

[11] Does a spring send forth fresh water and bitter from the same opening? [12] Can a fig tree, my brethren, bear olives, or a grapevine bear figs? Thus no spring yields both salt water and fresh. [13] Who is wise and understanding among you? Let him show by good conduct that his works are done in the meekness of wisdom. [14] But if you have bitter envy and self-seeking in your hearts, do not boast and lie against the

truth. [15] This wisdom does not descend from above, but is earthly, sensual, demonic. [16] For where envy

and self-seeking exist, confusion and every evil thing are there. [17] But the wisdom that is from above is

first pure, then peaceable, gentle, willing to yield, full of mercy and good fruits, without partiality and

without hypocrisy. [18] Now the fruit of righteousness is sown in peace by those who make peace. (NKJV).

DISCOVER

By now you know a lot about James, and if you have taken the **Devote** and **Disciple** steps seriously, you realize that James knows a lot about you. That is, James is an expert at exposing human folly and of clarifying God's blueprint for our lives. This present section is no exception. In James 3:10-18, James contrasts the so-called wisdom of man with the life-giving wisdom of God. It is your task to *dis*-cover the timeless truths of this passage by creating some Helping Questions. The following are a few questions that will *un*-cover (Do you still remember the Greek word for "truth"?) the essential facts of James' message.

But first carefully read and reread the text. Become thoroughly familiar with the content of the passage before going on to the sample questions set forth below.

Sample Helping Questions

- Where has James previously mentioned the theme of wisdom in his epistle?

ANSWER

- How do the first three verses of this section (3:10-12) relate to what James has said in the previous lesson (3:1-9)?

ANSWER

- How might 3:10-12 relate to the issue of faith mentioned in 1:6-7?

ANSWER

_____

_____

_____

_____

_____

_____

You are now quite proficient in developing the five W's and one H questions (Who? What? When? Where? Why? and How?). Proceed to develop some good questions that will pry out the facts of James 3:10-18. Write out your questions and answers next.

MY HELPING QUESTIONS AND ANSWERS

_____

_____

_____

_____

_____

MY HELPING QUESTIONS AND ANSWERS CONTINUED

Here are a few more Helping Questions that will draw forth the essential data of this passage:

- Where has James previously mentioned "boasting" in his epistle? (List the verses in the space provided.)

ANSWER

- How do all of these verses compare? How are they different from one another?

ANSWER

- What connection might 3:14 have with 4:13-17?

ANSWER

Now you are to reread all of your Helping Questions and Answers. Sift out all of the facts and special aspects of the passage that have surfaced in the **Discover** step of IBS. Write down your observations here.

MY FINDINGS

 # DISCERN

Your grasp of the essential facts contained in James 3:10-18 has greatly increased due to your use of the Helping Questions. All that you have learned thus far will be put to good use in the **Discern** step of IBS. That is, your knowledge of the content of this passage will soon result in an *informed* interpretation of the Scriptures. Yet, as you have already learned by now, knowledge of the facts at hand is not the same thing as understanding the true *meaning* of the Bible. As the apostle Paul counsels:

> *For who among men knows the thoughts of a man except the man's spirit within him? In the same way no one knows the thoughts of God except the Spirit of God. We have not received the spirit of the world but the Spirit who is from God, that we may understand what God has freely given us. This is what we speak, not in words taught us by human wisdom but in words taught by the Spirit, expressing spiritual truths in spiritual words. The man without the Spirit does not accept the things that come from the Spirit of God, for they are foolishness to him, and he cannot understand them, because they are spiritually discerned* (1 Cor 2:11-14).

Paul's point is that only God understands God, and consequently only those who are filled with God's Spirit are able to *discern* the Word of God. So before attempting to arrive at an interpretation of this section, pray that the indwelling Spirit might reveal the heart of God to you.

PAUSE *for* PRAYER

"There is a way which seemeth right unto a man, but the end thereof are the ways of death" (Prov. 14:12 KJV). A carnal reliance upon one's own knowledge can be deadly. More souls have gone to hell thinking they were doing the right thing than we would care to know. That is why James is so aggressive in his message. His love for souls leads him to speak forcefully to the things that lead to death. As Jude warns, "Be merciful to those who doubt; snatch others from the fire and save them; to others show mercy, mixed with fear—hating even the clothing stained by corrupted flesh" (Jude 1:22-23). Pray that God not only allow your eyes *to see* the wisdom contained in this passage, but also that He empower you *to embrace* the wisdom contained in this passage.

As you get out all of your marking pens and pencils, review the marking system that you have employed to this point. James continues to present strong contrasts and vivid word-pictures throughout 3:10-18. You might want to incorporate some new symbols like A+ for godly wisdom and F- for carnal or worldly wisdom. Be creative and consistent for this will help you arrive at a solid interpretation.

The following notes will guide you along through the **Discern** step:

- Note the presence of the word "mouth" in 3:10. James is clearly still concerned with sin-filled speech in this section.

- Could one legitimately draw lines of connection between "mouth" in 3:10 and the word-picture of a spring of water in 3:11?

- The word for "bitter" in 3:11 (KJV) is the same word for "bitter" in 3:14. What kind of connection is James making here?

- The image of "coming down" used in 3:15, 17 is the same as used in 1:17. Can you signify comparisons here?

- You may want to connect 3:15 with what has already been said in 3:6.

Now work through the passage carefully—marking, highlighting, and inserting symbols where helpful. Especially note the extreme contrasts that James uses throughout this section. Also, give special effort to point out connections between this portion of James and other parts you have already interpreted.

➡PULLING IT ALL TOGETHER⬅

You have gathered many facts and taken note of many features in James 3:10-18. Your Helping Questions and Helping Tools have served you well. Now is the time to harvest the rich fruit of your labor. Study all of the answers and notations that you have made, and work toward coordinating them into one, unified interpretation. It is important to integrate all of your findings into a single, harmonious expression of meaning. Do not rush through your Helping Tools. Examine each color, underlining, and symbol, and jot down its interpretive significance. If you continue to take your time with the Helping Tools, you will be amazed at the extraordinary features that will emerge from the Word of God.

The following points will help you blend all of your *dis*-coverings into a smooth and sensible rendering of this passage. Write out your responses in the spaces provided.

- In what terms does James describe the wise person? Does he do so in terms of what one knows or of what one does?

ANSWER

- In light of your answer to this first point, how does this relate to 2:14-26?

ANSWER

- Where in the Scriptures do you find words and images similar to 3:17-18 (see Gal. 5:22-23)? What is the spiritual significance here?

ANSWER

Your responses to these last questions have no doubt got you thinking in the right direction. Now prayerfully gather up everything that has been revealed to you in this study and write out your interpretation below.

MY INTERPRETATION

MY INTERPRETATION CONTINUED

_____

_____

_____

_____

_____

_____

_____

_____

_____

_____

DEVO✝E

If James is anything, he is consistent. From the first verse until now, the apostle has challenged his readers at every turn. There is no jogging in place for James! It's all forward march! This is the intent of the **Devote** step of IBS. We are to "march into" the message of James with faith and power. Or as Peter taught, "To this you were called, because Christ suffered for you, leaving you an example, that you should follow in his steps" (1 Peter 2:21). This is the point in the study where you *commit* to walk in the steps that James has laid out for you.

135

You may want to take out your journal and "map out" the path that you commit to in this lesson. In this way, when the going gets tough, you can stay on track. If you write things down in your journal, even if you get sidetracked for a while, you'll know where to take up the journey again.

Yet no spiritual progress is of any value unless God leads the way. The kinds of expectations James sets forth in 3:10-18 cannot be met without the power of prayer.

PAUSE *for* PRAYER

In John 15:5, Jesus said, "I am the vine; you are the branches. If a man remains in me and I in him, he will bear much fruit; apart from me you can do nothing." The point here is clear: without a vital connection to Jesus, we can make no real progress in the Kingdom. Take a moment to strengthen that vital connection to the Lord.; for without it, you can do nothing.

The following questions and comments can help spur you along the path of commitment and obedience. Prayerfully read each one and be open to its role in your life.

- How often has there been an inconsistency between how we relate to God in worship and how we relate to others in life (James 3:10-12)?

- In the midst of our "winner takes all" society, do you really view *humility* as wisdom (James 3:13)?

- Have you ever taken pride in an accomplishment that was totally about you, and you thought, *I am a pretty smart person!* (James 3:14-15)?

More than likely, the Spirit has brought many other things to mind as you immersed your heart and mind in James 3:10-18. Sincerely seek God's help in making James' moral vision a reality in your everyday life.

⊕⟨✗⟩DISCIPLE

The **Disciple** step is all about deciding to take action on what we have learned. James' expectations are rich and substantial. Yet we can take heart in the words of the apostle Paul when he states, "For it is God who works in you to will and to act according to his good purpose" (Phil. 2:13). This means that in some mysterious way, when we step out in faith in obedience to His Word, the Spirit floods in and empowers us to do God's will. With that in mind, prayerfully take up the following challenges and seek to make them part of who you are.

With the help of God and through the power of the Holy Spirit, *this week . . .*

- I refuse to worship God if I have spoken ill of my brother or sister. Only after I make things right with my neighbor will I enter into worship again (Matt. 5:23-24).

- I commit to leave off selfish ambition by examining my motives and then bringing everything into line with the calling that God has placed on my life.

- I will become wise, not in my own eyes, but in the eyes of the Lord (Prov. 3:7). I will acquire the wisdom that is pleasing to God by acting on the virtues listed in James 3:17.

- I commit to resolving conflict and defusing tensions. In this way, I will acquire the wisdom that comes from being a peacemaker for God (James 4:18).

What a great change would happen if we could disciple at least one person in the kind of wisdom that James teaches in this lesson! Pray that God give you the opportunity to mentor another in the extraordinary gift of divine wisdom. Indeed, the Scriptures state, "Wisdom is supreme; therefore get wisdom. Though it cost all you have, get understanding" (Prov. 4:7). So be prepared this week to gently but faithfully disciple another in the kind of wisdom that "comes down from heaven" (James 3:17).

A PENTECOSTAL APPROACH to BIBLE STUDY

LESSON SEVEN

James

4:1-8

REAL FAITH
IS NOT WORLDLY

L E S S O N   S E V E N

James 4:1-8

Real Faith Is Not Worldly

KEY VERSE

You adulterous people, don't you know that friendship with the world is hatred toward God? **(James 4:4).**

Introduction

In this section James is getting at the heart of the matter. That is, all of the many problems that have arisen among "the twelve tribes . . . scattered abroad" (James 1:1 KJV) stem from one major sin: worldliness. A lack of true wisdom (1:5; 3:13-18), doubt (1:6), blaming God for temptation (1:12-18), a lifeless faith (1:19-25; 2:14-26), favoring the rich (2:1-13), and sinful speech (3:1-12) all find their source in befriending the world and not truly loving God. James' point is that a carnal rebellious spirit is completely contrary to the Spirit of God. The only way forward for James' recipients is to humble themselves before God and resist the devil (4:6-7), draw near to God (4:8), and in due season, God will

141

give them grace (4:6). Then, and only then, will God exalt them to their rightful place in the Kingdom (4:10).

What James is advocating, indeed what he has been promoting since the beginning of his epistle, is commitment to life in the Spirit. He is demanding that his recipients receive the gifts of God (1:17) and evidence the fruit of the Spirit (3:17-18). All of this requires a lifestyle of prayer (1 Thess. 5:17). So before launching into this exciting and supremely challenging part of James, take a moment to pray for God's guidance.

PAUSE for PRAYER

The only antidote to worldliness is godliness. No amount of man-made virtue or moral discipline can break the stranglehold of the world on a person's life. The apostle John says the same thing: "Do not love the world or anything in the world. If anyone loves the world, the love of the Father is not in him. For everything in the world—the cravings of sinful man, the lust of his eyes and the boasting of what he has and does—comes not from the Father but from the world" (1 John 2:15-16). God is a jealous God in the sense that He is completely devoted to you and so desires that you be completely devoted to Him. Anything less than complete commitment to God is spiritual adultery; it is the spirit of idolatry (James 4:4-5; Ezek. 6:9; 23:30, 37). Pray that by the time you have finished this lesson, every aspect of your life is totally surrendered to God. Pray that your mind, your heart, and your actions demonstrate complete fidelity to Him.

 # THE TEXT

James 4:1-8

¹What causes fights and quarrels among you? Don't they come from your desires that battle within you? ² You want something but don't get it. You kill and covet, but you cannot have what you want. You quarrel and fight. You do not have, because you do not ask God. ³ When you ask, you do not receive, because you ask with wrong motives, that you may spend what you get on your pleasures. ⁴ You adulterous people, don't you know that friendship with the world is hatred toward God? Anyone who chooses to be a friend of the world becomes an enemy of God. ⁵ Or do you think Scripture says without

reason that the spirit he caused to live in us envies intensely? [6] But he gives us more grace. That is why

Scripture says: "God opposes the proud but gives grace to the humble." [7] Submit yourselves, then, to

God. Resist the devil, and he will flee from you. [8] Come near to God and he will come near to you. Wash

your hands, you sinners, and purify your hearts, you double-minded.

DISCOVER

James 4:1-8 is a very rich text. There are so many "echoes" of the Old Testament prophets in this passage of Scripture. Also, there are many references to the teachings of Jesus. So you need to carefully read through these eight verses. As you read, you may want to jot down scriptures that come to mind. As will become apparent, you will engage James at one point, but soon his powerful words will lead you on a journey throughout God's holy Word!

Because there is so much in this passage, you will have to really work to "pry out facts" as you read along. There is a lot to *dis*-cover in this passage, but it is going to take a lot of work on your part. The careful crafting of Helping Questions will become especially important in this section. A few sample questions are listed below to get you started. After you answer these questions, you will be given the chance to develop your own questions.

Sample Helping Questions

- How might the "desires" mentioned in 4:1 relate to the special words and images set forth in 1:14-15?

ANSWER

- What words of Jesus are called to mind after reading James 4:2-3?

ANSWER

- Who in the New Testament might be described as a "friend of the world and enemy of God" (see Matt. 26:14-16; 2 Tim. 4:10)?

ANSWER

Now carefully study through James 4:1-8 again, and create your own Helping Questions. Take care to make questions that will really pull forth the essential data of the text. You'll need all of the information you can get to arrive at an informed interpretation in the Discern step below. So write out some good questions and answer them in the space provided.

MY HELPING QUESTIONS AND ANSWERS

MY HELPING QUESTIONS AND ANSWERS CONTINUED

Here are a couple more questions that will help to *dis*-cover the facts contained in James 4:1-8.

- How do you think the word "spirit" should be translated in 4:5? Should it be spelled with a lowercase s̲ or with a capital S̲?

ANSWER

- What other scriptures can you cite that would complement or agree with James 4:7?

ANSWER

All of your hard work in the **Discover** step of IBS has brought forth many interesting facts and features of James 4:1-8. Reread all of your questions and answers and sift out all of the data that will help you make a solid interpretation of this important passage of Scripture. Write out your findings next.

MY FINDINGS

MY FINDINGS CONTINUED

DISCERN

Your summary work in gathering up the facts of James 4:1-8 will be put to good use in the **Discern** step. Here you will focus not on just what the text says, but will concentrate on what the text means. So gather up all of your marking pens and pencils and look for key words, repeated phrases, special images, and the like. Make use of striking symbols again that will fix the meaning of the text in your mind. For example, James includes a lot of words about fighting and battling. Perhaps a pair of boxing gloves ( ) could stand in for all of the aggressive and negative images that James uses in this passage. Once again, James addresses some real strongholds in our lives. Indeed, there is a kind of fight that is pleasing to God—our fight against the devil and all that he stands for. Certainly this is an area that we can all pray about.

PAUSE *for* PRAYER

In Ephesians 6:12-17, Paul states:

> *For our struggle is not against flesh and blood, but against the rulers, against the authorities, against the powers of this dark world and against the spiritual forces of evil in the heavenly realms. Therefore put on the full armor of God, so that when the day of evil comes, you may be able to stand your ground, and after you have done everything, to stand. Stand firm then, with the belt of truth*

buckled around your waist, with the breastplate of righteousness in place, and with your feet fitted with the readiness that comes from the gospel of peace. In addition to all this, take up the shield of faith, with which you can extinguish all the flaming arrows of the evil one. Take the helmet of salvation and the sword of the Spirit, which is the word of God.

Paul's words here teach us many things. Yet the central message of this passage is that the real source behind all strife and violence is the devil and all of his evil helpers. So it is the devil and his minions that we should be fighting against and not against ourselves.

In setting forth this image of spiritual warfare, Paul paints the image of a Roman soldier in full battle gear. Each piece of armor is symbolic of the spiritual weapons that the believer has at his or her disposal. Let us pray that we can make full use of the weapons that God has granted us to fight the real enemy, who is Satan.

You will find some tips for interpretation listed below. These interpretive "hints" can strengthen the insights that you have already gained by way of the **Discover** step. These "clues" will also assist you in the development of your Helping Tools. They may well bring certain colors, marks or symbols to mind as you work through the passage again.

- The word for "desires" in James 4:1 is *hedonē*, from which we get the English word *hedonism*. *Hedonism* means the unbridled pursuit of bodily pleasures, especially of a sinful kind.

- The words "kill" and "covet" (4:2) should probably be taken metaphorically. In other words, "kill" and "covet" refer to sins of the heart like hatred and lust (see Matt 5:21-22).

- With the mention of "kill" and "covet," James seems to have the Ten Commandments in mind. In stating that God is a jealous God (James 4:5), what other commandment might James have in mind?

- The phrase "the Spirit that dwells in you" (see 4:5) sounds a lot like something Paul would write. What scriptures in Paul's writings emphasize the indwelling of the Spirit?

- Note that the word for "double-minded" in 4:8 is the same word used in 1:8.

There is so much more in these verses. So continue to make notes, symbols, and interpretive marks in the passage supplied above.

➡PULLING IT ALL TOGETHER⬅

By way of your Helping Questions and Helping Tools, the deep truths of James 4:1-8 have been *un*-covered (Do you still remember the literal meaning of "revelation"?). Go back now and restudy all of the insights that have surfaced as a result of the **Discover** and **Discern** steps of IBS. Examine each of your color codes from the beginning of the passage until the end. Jot down notes concerning the significance of each sequence of colors, highlighting, or underlining. Allow the frequency of words, their placement in the text, and their relationship to other parts of James to speak meaning into your heart. Indeed, it is time to integrate all of the facts and meanings that have come forth from your work and weave all of these items into one, cohesive, informed interpretation of the text. The following questions and comments will help you formulate a solid rendering of this passage:

- Rhetorical questions are a writing technique designed to draw forth a particular answer. Read the rhetorical questions found in James 4:1, 2, 4-5. What kinds of answers do you think James expects to these questions?

ANSWER

- Making "black and white" contrasts is another way of emphasizing a point. Identify the different kinds of contrasts found in James 4:1-8. What are some of the points that James is making by use of these contrasts?

ANSWER

- Although by necessity, James must mention some really negative things in this passage, list the positive comments he makes and their meanings beginning with James 4:6-8.

ANSWER

By now you should be confident as to the meaning of James 4:1-8. Review all of the good points that have come to light as a result of your hard work on this passage. You are now prepared to answer the all-important question, "What does James 4:1-8 mean?" Write out your interpretation of this section in the space provided below.

MY INTERPRETATION

MY INTERPRETATION CONTINUED

DEVO┼E

James 4:1-8 is particularly relevant to the **Devote** step of IBS. This step calls for personal *commitment* and *wholehearted* obedience. The **Devote** step means moving in God's direction. It means truly wanting to do God's will. It means desiring friendship with God so much more than desiring friendship with the world. Or, as James clearly states, "Submit yourselves, then, to God. Resist the devil, and he will flee from you. [8] Come near to God and he will come near to you. Wash your hands, you sinners, and purify your hearts, you double-minded" (James 4:7-8).

James' challenge of drawing near to God will only come to pass with prayer. Therefore, prepare your heart to receive James' message by taking a moment to seek God's guidance in prayer.

PAUSE *for* PRAYER

The psalmist states, "As the deer pants for streams of water, so my soul pants for you, O God. My soul thirsts for God, for the living God. When can I go and meet with God?" (Ps. 42:1-2). In other words, the psalmist's desire to meet with God, to draw near to God, was the same as a thirsting deer's desire to get a drink of cold water in a dry and weary land. Do you have that same burning desire to draw near to God? Are you willing to seek Him in prayer so that you might receive His grace (James 4:6)? Are you willing to draw so near to God that the devil can't stand to be near you? Are you longing

156

to have everything that you do and say be sanctified for God's work and to have your heart purified by His Holy Spirit?

The following comments and questions may grant you some "structure" for drawing near to God. As you respond to this section, you may want to write out the kinds of commitments you are making to the Lord. These journal entries can serve as your written "covenant" to follow through on your spiritual pledges to God.

- In the light of what James says in 4:1-2, would you describe yourself as a peacemaker or a fighter?

- In making your requests to God, how easy is it for you to pray, "Not my will be done, but Your will be done"?

- On a scale from 1 to 10, with 1 being no friendship with the world and 10 being in love with the world, what number would you assign yourself right now?

- On a scale from 1 to 10, with 1 being no friendship with God and 10 being an unqualified love for God, what number would you assign yourself right now?

- Which of the Ten Commandments have you recently broken, if not in fact, then in spirit?

⊕✝DISCIPLE

If the **Devote** step is all about spiritual movement on the inside, the **Disciple** step is all about realization of God's will on the outside. The critical point here is to determine in concrete terms exactly what God would have you to do in light of James 4:1-8. In other words, how can I "incarnate"

157

or "make real" the teachings of James in my life? The following will help you take real steps in real time to "submit yourself to God" (see James 4:7) and "come near to God" (James 4:8).

This week, with God's help, I commit to . . .

- Not speaking or acting in a "warlike" or "aggressive" manner (James 4:1-2).

- Not asking for a single thing for myself in prayer. All my prayers will be in praise to God or will be genuinely seeking the welfare of others (James 4:3).

- Breaking off my "engagement" to the world. God will know that I am only in love with Him (James 4:4-5).

- Submitting everything to God, whatever it takes, so that I can draw near to Him and receive grace and cleansing (James 4:8).

As daunting as these personal challenges may be, the Lord gives us the even more daunting task of discipling others in the ways of James. You may know of a brother or sister in Christ who is not only undermining their witness because of a quarrelsome spirit, they are gradually losing their joy as well. Pray that the Lord make a way for you to share this life-giving message of James with this person. Also—and this is a sensitive issue as well—you may know of a self-righteous believer who feels that they have not broken any of God's commandments. Ironically, James indicates that such persons are proud and have cut themselves off from God's grace. They have distanced themselves from the purifying mercy of the Lord (James 4:6-8). If God creates the spiritual context for you to share this portion of James with them, you must have the courage to do so. In this way you may well turn away disaster in their lives (Prov. 11:30).

A PENTECOSTAL APPROACH
to
BIBLE STUDY

LESSON EIGHT

James

4:9-17

REAL FAITH
SUBMITS TO GOD

LESSON EIGHT
James 4:9-17
Real Faith Submits to God

 ## KEY VERSE

Anyone, then, who knows the good he ought to do and doesn't do it, sins **(James 4:17).**

Introduction

The prophetic voice of James really comes through in this passage! As the great prophet Micah preached, "Because of this I will weep and wail; I will go about barefoot and naked. I will howl like a jackal and moan like an owl" (Mic. 1:8) so too does James. Similarly, in the spirit of Lamentations, James exhorts, "Grieve, mourn, and wail!" (James 4:9). The language of James in this section can leave no doubt that for James, the dreadful "Day of the Lord" has finally arrived (Joel 2:31; 3:14). This is the same kind of warning preached by Isaiah. He exhorted, "Wail, for the day of the Lord is near; it will come like destruction from the Almighty" (Isa. 13:6). The only real option we have is to humbly repent in the face of God's impending judgment. Then, and only then, will God forgive and lift us up to a state of honor.

The seriousness of James' message moves us to prayer. This is true because James demands change. He wants evil speech and behavior to cease. He firmly believes that *knowledge* of what is good requires the *doing* of what is good.

This would be an opportune time to pray that God would truly grant us a spirit of repentance so that we could receive all the good things that He has for us.

PAUSE *for*  PRAYER

"Search me, O God, and know my heart; test me and know my anxious thoughts. See if there is any offensive way in me, and lead me in the way everlasting" (Ps. 139:23-24). This is the prayer of humility. This is the kind of prayer that leads to the path of divine favor. James requires that we pray this kind of prayer. Enter now into heart-felt prayer, seeking God's divine direction as you commence this important lesson.

THE TEXT

James 4:9-17

[9]Grieve, mourn and wail. Change your laughter to mourning and your joy to gloom. [10] Humble yourselves before the Lord, and he will lift you up. [11] Brothers, do not slander one another. Anyone who

speaks against his brother or judges him speaks against the law and judges it. When you judge the law, you are not keeping it, but sitting in judgment on it. [12] There is only one Lawgiver and Judge, the one who is able to save and destroy. But you—who are you to judge your neighbor? [13] Now listen, you who say, "Today or tomorrow we will go to this or that city, spend a year there, carry on business and make money." [14] Why, you do not even know what will happen tomorrow. What is your life? You are a mist that appears for a little while and then vanishes. [15] Instead, you ought to say, "If it is the Lord's will, we will live and do this or that." [16] As it is, you boast and brag. All such boasting is evil. [17] Anyone, then, who knows the good he ought to do and doesn't do it, sins.

DISCOVER

The first task here is to read the text *with a purpose*. That is, intentionally study this passage to isolate the content of James, to identify controlling ideas, and to note connections with areas of James that you have already studied. You will soon find that the language and imagery in this section are so powerful that it will be easy to develop some Helping Questions. That is, the prophetic tone and vivid word pictures contained in James 4:9-17 bring to mind many relevant questions and answers. In fact, you will have to be very selective in the choice of your Helping Questions. Only craft those questions that get at the heart of James' message. The following are a few sample questions that will highlight some of the issues that James is grappling with in these verses.

Sample Helping Questions

- Why would James want his recipients to change their laughter into mourning and their joy into sadness (4:9)?

ANSWER

- Where else in Scripture have you read that if a person humbles himself or herself before the Lord, then God will lift them up (James 4:10)?

ANSWER

- Where else in James does he address evil speaking (4:11)?

ANSWER

- How can James say that if we judge another person, then we are actually judging the Law?

ANSWER

Just these few questions have helped you realize the complexity of James' thought in 4:9-17. He has made some real connections between a false worldview (laughing and rejoicing when they should be mourning and weeping (4:9)], the misuse of speech (4:11) and questioning the power of the Law to judge properly (4:11-12). Admittedly, these are some fairly abstract concepts! However, the rest of this passage (vv. 13-17) deals with more concrete issues related to right and wrong behavior. So carefully read through this section again and make up some Helping Questions of your own.

MY HELPING QUESTIONS & ANSWERS

Here are a few more Helping Questions that will draw forth the data of this powerful section of the Word. These questions will *dis*-cover the truth of what is conveyed here.

- How might you describe the attitude of the persons addressed in 4:13?

ANSWER

- What words of Jesus come to mind when you read, "Why you do not even know what will happen tomorrow" (4:14)?

ANSWER

- Where else in James has he spoken of "boasting" (4:16)?

ANSWER

Your development of Helping Questions has provided "shape" to your thoughts on James. Reread all of your questions and answers and summarize all of the findings, ideas, and facts that have come to light on this passage. Write out all that you have learned in the space provided.

MY FINDINGS

MY FINDINGS CONTINUED

 # DISCERN

You have *un*-covered a lot of facts and important concepts of James 4:9-17 by way of the Helping Questions. This knowledge of what the text *says* has empowered you to interpret what the text *means*. That is, you have enough information and understanding to interpret this important passage of Scripture.

In order to coordinate your ideas and to "dig out" even more data from James, you will now develop and use a number of Helping Tools. You will again highlight, underline, and use symbols to note special words, concepts, and features of this passage. Remember to reuse marking methods that might apply to the text at hand. In other words, if you used a certain color or symbol to represent improper speech in 3:1-12, use that same color or symbol to mark evil speech in 4:11. The same holds true for repeated themes like "money" (see 1:9-11; 2:1-7; 4:13) and "boasting" (1:9-11; 3:5,14).

The **Discern** step is arguably the most important part of IBS. Everything has led up to this task of interpretation. Ask God now to help you plumb the depths of James' words in 4:9-17.

PAUSE *for* PRAYER

In 2 Samuel 22:29 we read, "For thou art my lamp, O Lord: and the Lord will lighten my darkness" (KJV). This scripture teaches that we cannot approach the Bible just like any other piece of literature. If the Bible is inspired by God, only God can reveal its true meaning. So without the help of the Spirit, you will never arrive at the true sense and impact of James 4:9-17. Pray now that God will enliven the Spirit within you so that you might *discern* what the Lord is saying in this passage.

Here are some additional helps that will guide you to a sound rendering of this scripture passage.

- A reading of 1 Peter 5:6 will give you additional insight into James 4:10.

- Paul's words in Romans 2:1-3; 2:17-23 sound a lot like James 4:11-12.

- James' emphasis on "doing" in 4:17 echoes a central theme of James found in 2:14-26.

➡PULLING IT ALL TOGETHER⬅

You now have become thoroughly familiar with many facts and features of James 4:9-17. Review all that you have learned from your Helping Questions and Helping Tools. The following comments and questions will help you integrate the information and meaning that you have been able to derive thus far. Again, give your Helping Tools a chance to reveal God's truth to you. It takes some effort to examine each of the marking tools you have created and to *discern* its significance. Yet this is time well spent! There are few things more exciting than being "surprised" by new insights into God's Word, and Helping Tools have a way of wonderfully surprising us in our study of the Bible.

- Who might James have in mind when he says, "There is only one Lawgiver" (James 4:12)?

ANSWER

- James' point in 4:15 reflects the doctrine of the *sovereignty* of God, or the belief that God is in control of all things. How might the business plans of some of James' recipients reflect poorly on the doctrine of divine sovereignty?

ANSWER

At this point you are more than prepared to write out a responsible interpretation of James 4:9-17. In the light of all you have learned, write out your interpretation below.

MY INTEPRETATION

MY INTEPRETATION CONTINUED

_____

_____

_____

_____

_____

_____

_____

_____

_____

_____

DEVOTE

As a result of your careful study of James 4:9-17, you have a clear understanding of what this passage means. You have an equally clear understanding of what James expcts of his readers. In other words, you know exactly what kind of obedience and commitment is required of anyone who takes this scripture seriously.

The **Devote** step of IBS is designed to help you make this kind of commitment. It is intended to serve as a clear signpost pointing you to sincere obedience to God's Word. You know too that the kinds of spiritual challenges presented in James are not to be taken lightly. They are the kinds of discipleship goals that can only be reached by way of prayer.

PAUSE *for* PRAYER

King David was a man who knew what it meant to rejoice in the Lord! At times he would sing and dance in the presence of his God. In Psalm 9:2 he shouts, "I will be glad and rejoice in you; I will sing praise to your name, O Most High." Yet David also knew how to lament and mourn before the Lord. In another psalm he cries, "I am worn out from groaning; all night long I flood my bed with weeping and drench my couch with tears" (Ps. 6:6). His son Solomon must have observed the ebb and flow of David's spirit when he wrote, "There is a time for everything . . . a time to weep and a time to laugh, a time to mourn and a time to dance" (Eccl. 3:1, 4). For James, it is a time to lament . . . to weep . . . to mourn. James exhorts this season of sorrow because his readers are out of touch with what time it is. It is not time to be frivolous and lighthearted. It is time for some serious soul-searching and intercession. Are you prepared to lay aside a spirit of mirth and embrace a somber time of reflection before the Lord? The following comments and questions can help you along this mature *Path to Discipleship.*

- James' prohibition against slander is not simply concerned with speaking ill of others (James 4:11-12). He is after something much deeper than that. To judge someone is to take on the role of the Law of God. By extension, then, to stand in judgment of someone is to stand in the place of God! This is the arch sin of the devil (Isa. 14:13-14). James knows this, and this is why he commands his readers to weep and lament. Perhaps you too—if not on purpose maybe unconsciously—have severely judged another person. Pray now that God will grant you the wisdom and power to resist such judgments and leave that job to God and His Law!

- The second great sin that James addresses in this section is the sin of presumption (James 4:13-14). This is the sin of thinking we are in complete control of our destiny. This is the sin that denies the sovereign control of the Almighty. In making your plans for tomorrow, do you always say, "If the Lord wills . . . " or do you thoughtlessly push ahead as if God doesn't matter? Examine your heart now and renounce any sin of presumption.

- The third great sin that James confronts is the sin of omission (James 4:17). The very nature of this sin practically guarantees that it will go unnoticed! Nevertheless, James says that if we know to do good and yet do not do it, then this is a sin. Has the Spirit ever revealed to you something good that you should do, and for some reason or other, you failed to do it? Pray now for the kind of spiritual sensitivity that will move you to action when you know to do good.

✝ ΙΧΘΥΣ DISCIPLE

The **Devote** step of IBS addresses the heart. The **Disciple** step addresses our hands and feet.

That is, this aspect of our study calls for concrete, observable change in our behavior. So if you have

sincerely devoted yourself to the spiritual counsel of James in this section, you are prepared to make

definitive changes in your life. Therefore, make a covenant with the Word and commit to the following

call to action.

This week, I commit to . . .

- Stop judging others. I will let the Law do its job, and I will let God alone be God.

- Renouncing the sin of presumption in my life. I commit to putting God back on the throne of my life and always seeking His will in everything that I say and do.

- *Immediately and without hesitation* doing what I know to be good.

As challenging as James might be to us personally, his words are even more challenging to share with others. Nevertheless, when we truly commit to discipling others, at times "tough love" is required. It is no fun—but if you really care for someone, and you enjoy the kind of relationship that permits "iron to sharpen iron" (see Prov. 27:17), then James' counsel in 4:9-17 may be just what is needed. Perhaps there is someone in your circle of influence that just doesn't know when to be serious. They resist that hard, long look within, the kind of self-examination that James calls for. Prayerfully seek an opportunity to disciple this loved one in the teachings of James. Yet again, you may know someone who loves the Lord, but simply does not make a habit of submitting their plans to God. How much more blessed they would be if they could be discipled in this regard! Finally, someone you know may have planned to do some good thing but, for some reason, has just not followed through (see 2 Cor. 8:10-11; 9:1-2). God may use you to inspire that friend to complete that good work they had previously committed to do.

In the final chapter of James, he speaks to something that is not only important to us as individuals, but is essential to the strength of any nation. As the Scriptures state, "Righteousness exalts a nation, but sin is a disgrace to any people" (Prov. 14:34). In a similar way, in his concluding chapter to "the twelve tribes scattered among the nations" (James 1:1), James exhorts his recipients to be honest and fair in business.

LESSON NINE

James

5:1-9

REAL FAITH
SEEKS JUSTICE

LESSON NINE

James 5:1-9

Real Faith Seeks Justice

 ## KEY VERSE

Be patient, then, brothers, until the Lord's coming. See how the farmer waits for the land to yield its valuable crop and how patient he is for the autumn and spring rains. You too, be patient and stand firm, because the Lord's coming is near (James 5:7-8).

Introduction

The opening verses of this section address the second coming of Jesus. In a way, the Second Coming has been in the background of much of what James has said throughout his epistle. The temporal nature of riches (1:9-11) and all of His words concerning judgment (2:12-13; 4:7-12, 14) assume the second coming of Jesus. In the same way, James' emphasis on end-time rewards (1:12) looks forward to the time when Jesus comes again. In this sense, James is in perfect harmony with the rest of the New Testament which teaches that eschatology (the study of the end times and the Second Coming) cannot be separated from ethics (personal behavior). In short, the message of James is that each of us will give account of our lives at the Second Coming, so we need to live right in the present.

Once again, James is in complete agreement with his Lord and half-brother, Jesus. Many of Jesus' parables, such as the parable of the ten virgins (Matt. 25:1-13) and the parable of the talents (Matt. 25:14-30) teach that one needs to live righteously in the present, because we don't know when we will give account to the Judge.

Also in this section, James once again returns to the theme of the rich and the poor (1:10-11; 2:1-10; 4:13-16). He has already addressed three main problems in this area: worldly materialism (1:10-11; 4:13-16), favoritism toward the rich (2:1-5, 8-9), and economic oppression of the poor (2:6-7). In 5:1-9, James returns again to this last category of the rich tyrannizing the poor.

As you work through this portion of James, it might help to keep two things in mind. First, many of the economic protections that we enjoy today were nonexistent in the first-century world. There was no Department of Commerce, no antitrust laws, no Better Business Bureau, no unemployment benefits, no Social Security . . . you get the picture. For the most part, nonskilled workers were at the mercy of the rich (see Matt. 20:1-16). The lack of surplus money affected many aspects of the poor, including adequate representation before the law. As was the case with the apostle Paul when he appeared before Felix, the common person didn't have the money to hire an expensive lawyer like Tertullus (Acts 24:1-2). This explains why James comes down so hard on those who cheat and oppress the poor in 5:1-9. An appeal to common decency and fairness in business was the only hope that the poor had in this world.

Yet for believers, there was another hope for justice: Judgment Day. This is the second point to keep in mind as you study James 5:1-9. For James, the hope of the Second Coming includes a strong element of justice. All the wrongs done in this world, especially the injustices done to people who did not have the means to defend themselves—all of these "sins of finance," so to speak, *will be judged*. This truth helps to explain James' harsh tone in this section. He has a passion for fairness, a passion that seeks justice each and every day until the Second Coming!

So much sorrow in our individual lives and in the life of our nation could be avoided if we simply did the right thing. Let's pray that God grants us a passion for fairness that does the right thing in every instance and for each and every person, regardless of their social and economic status.

PAUSE *for* PRAYER

The psalmist prayed, "A father to the fatherless, a defender of widows, is God in his holy dwelling" (Ps. 68:5). This is the heart of God! He is a defender of those who in this world have no defense. On the other hand, He is the Judge of all those who take advantage of the weak. As Isaiah prophesied, "The Lord enters into judgment against the elders and leaders of his people: 'It is you who have ruined my vineyard; the plunder from the poor is in your houses. What do you mean by crushing my people and grinding the faces of the poor?' declares the Lord, the Lord Almighty" (Isa. 3:14-15).

As you enter into this intense portion of James, pray now that you always find yourself on the right side of justice, that is, standing on the side of the Lord.

 # THE TEXT

James 5:1-9

¹Now listen, you rich people, weep and wail because of the misery that is coming upon you. ² Your wealth

has rotted, and moths have eaten your clothes. ³ Your gold and silver are corroded. Their corrosion will

testify against you and eat your flesh like fire. You have hoarded wealth in the last days. ⁴ Look! The

wages you failed to pay the workmen who mowed your fields are crying out against you. The cries of

the harvesters have reached the ears of the Lord Almighty. ⁵ You have lived on earth in luxury and self-

indulgence. You have fattened yourselves in the day of slaughter. ⁶ You have condemned and murdered

innocent men, who were not opposing you. ⁷ Be patient, then, brothers, until the Lord's coming. See

how the farmer waits for the land to yield its valuable crop and how patient he is for the autumn and spring rains. [8] You too, be patient and stand firm, because the Lord's coming is near. [9] Don't grumble against each other, brothers, or you will be judged. The Judge is standing at the door!

DISCOVER

The **Discover** step of IBS is to really dig out the facts of James' epistle. At this point in your study, this should be a relatively easy task. This is true because you know *a lot* of facts about James. This means that you have graduated from the level of a mere inquirer to the status of an informed reader. Everything you have dis-covered to this point has drawn you into the mind of James. In a sense, you are now able to think the thoughts of James. So in this **Discover** step, you are able to view the text through the "lenses" of James, so to speak. This can greatly help in arriving at a responsible interpretation of James 5:1-9. You understand the "tone" of James and now understand that his prophetic voice is passionate about justice and fairness. You know, too, that his confrontational style is not meant to harm but to heal.

So carefully read the assigned text, all the while seeking to arrive at what James is saying. The use of select Helping Questions will give some structure to your study and direct your inquiry more effectively. As usual, some sample Helping Questions have been supplied to open the way to a deeper understanding of this passage.

Sample Helping Questions

- Why would James tell the rich person in 1:10 to experience joyous pride but then in 5:1 command rich people to "weep and wail"?

ANSWER

- How might the "weeping and wailing" in 5:1 relate to the mourning in 4:9?

ANSWER

- What can you recall from the sayings of Jesus that sounds a lot like James' words in 5:2? In seeking to answer this question, the student is directed to study Jesus' "Sermon on the Mount" (Matt. 6:1-34).

ANSWER

You are quite skilled at creating questions that bring the facts of James to light. Read 5:1-9 again with an eye to making some select questions that really *un*-cover the content of this important passage in James.

MY HELPING QUESTIONS AND ANSWERS

MY HELPING QUESTIONS AND ANSWERS

Here are a few more questions that will draw out the important content of James:

- How might James 5:4 relate to the story of Abel in Genesis 4:10?

ANSWER

• Where in the Old Testament might we find the words "cries . . . have reached the ears of the Lord Almighty"?

ANSWER

• How might James' words in 5:7 compare with what Paul says in 2 Timothy 2:6?

ANSWER

- How might James' warning against "grumbling" and the impending judgment in 5:9 relate to the evils of the tongue in 3:1-12?

ANSWER

Now review all of the Helping Questions and your answers, then write out all of the facts that you have been able to *discover* in James 5:1-9.

MY HELPING QUESTIONS AND ANSWERS

My Helping Questions and Answers Continued

_____

_____

_____

_____

_____

_____

_____

_____

_____

_____

DISCERN

Your experience with IBS is really coming into play now. No doubt, even as you worked through the **Discover** step, you were already thinking of how you could color-code and mark special features found in James 5:1-9. Since you have already built up a considerable array of Helping Tools, you have much to choose from. Again you might want to choose some memorable symbols like **$$** for the many references to money and riches present in this passage. Also, you may resort to the symbol again to tag all the references to "judgment."

This challenging portion of James calls for a special season of prayer. His hard-hitting message has the goodness of divine judgment in sight. And God's judgment is good! For without God "balancing the books" so to speak, all of the evil and cruelty that has occurred in this life would go unaccounted for, and those who have been victimized and then robbed of justice would remain victimized for eternity. James says that this is not going to happen. As surely as God lives, the cries of the oppressed have been heard by the Lord God Almighty and He will avenge all wrongs.

As you enter into the **Discern** step of IBS, you must keep before your eyes the perfect justice of God.

PAUSE *for* PRAYER

Much of what James says in this text sounds like the prophet Micah. The "weep and wail" of James 5:1 sounds like Micah 1:10-11 (see also Joel 1:5). In the same way, James' passion for justice echoes the key verse of Micah 6:8: "He has showed you, O man, what is good. And what does the Lord require of you? To act justly and to love mercy and to walk humbly with your God." These three things—justice, mercy, and humility—encapsulate the burden of James in chapter 5. Pray now that the Spirit makes these three virtues the hallmark of your walk with the Lord.

The following comments may help you develop an effective marking system to *discern* the meaning of this section.

- The moth-eaten clothing spoken of in 5:2 spells the doom of the fine clothes mentioned in 2:2-3.

- In the ancient world, silver and gold thread would often be woven into clothing to show wealth and social status (see Acts 12:21-23). At times, though, this metal would corrode and ruin fancy apparel.

- All throughout 5:1-9, James has a courtroom scene in mind. This is why he speaks about corruption testifying against the rich in the Day of Judgment and ill-gotten gain crying out against evil landowners at the last day.

The word-pictures used by James in this section are striking! For this reason, you can take full advantage of the colors and symbols of your marking system. So think creatively, drawing upon what you have done in past lessons, but also develop new marking techniques for what James says in 5:1-9.

➡PULLING IT ALL TOGETHER⬅

Your careful work with the Helping Questions and the Helping Tools has *un*-covered many truths contained in James 5:1-9. Do not underestimate the power of your Helping Tools, especially in this section. Individually trace out each color and marking system and write down the interpretive insight that has come forth. All of this is contributing to your ability to "rightly divide" (see 2 Tim. 2:15 KJV) this special portion of James.

Having reviewed all of the facts that have surfaced by your use of Helping Questions and all the unique features revealed by your Helping Tools, write out a clear and substantial interpretation of James 5:1-9.

The following comments will help you coordinate your thoughts concerning this passage:

- What parables of Jesus condemn the hoarding of worldly wealth to the neglect of the riches of the kingdom of God? (One example is Luke 12:15-21.)

ANSWER

- What parts of the Sermon on the Mount reflect some of the themes found in James 5:1-9 (see Matt. 5:1–7:29; Luke 6:20-49)?

ANSWER

- Why would James compare overindulgent persons with a calf being fattened for the slaughter (James 5:5)?

ANSWER

Once again, review everything that has come to light in your study of James 5:1-9. As you revisit your findings, always keep this question before you: "What is *the meaning* of James' words in this challenging portion of scripture?" Having sufficiently answered that question, write out your interpretation now.

MY INTERPRETATION

MY INTERPRETATION CONTINUED

DEVO†E

The words of James can be penetrating. He does not "pull any punches" when confronting the injustices against the poor. It is not likely that any true believers can fully identify with what James says in 5:1-9. Yet God inspired these words for a purpose! To a lesser degree, but certainly to some degree, we all have let perfect justice fade from view. So, to some extent, we can appropriate James' challenge in this section. Let's pray for God's perfect will to speak through what James has to say here.

PAUSE *for* PRAYER

Once again, the words of James remind us of the prophet Hosea when he proclaimed, "Sow for yourselves righteousness, reap the fruit of unfailing love, and break up your unplowed ground; for it is time to seek the Lord, until he comes and showers righteousness on you" (Hos. 10:12). This combination of agricultural images and passion for God's righteousness is so typical of James. And so it is with James 5:1-9. There is economic injustice in the mowing of hayfields. There is a "calf" in the barn being fattened for the slaughter. And so the hearts of Hosea and James come together and lead us to prayer. They would have us to pray that we break up the hard soil of our souls, to sow seeds of righteousness, harvest the fruit of "mercy" (KJV) and await that divine "rain" (KJV) of righteousness.

The following comments are designed to help you hear God's voice in James 5:1-9. Some of what follows may not apply to you at all, but may bring other things to mind for you to pray about. As you read each entry, jot down your thoughts in your journal or logbook. This will help you formulate your understanding of what the Lord is saying to your heart.

- To what extent have material things of this world "eaten into" your service for the Kingdom?

- Has the drive to accumulate the riches of this world to some degree resulted in a poverty of spirit?

- Have you always put what is fair and equitable ahead of what is advantageous and profitable?

- In the light of what James has said in this section, would you feel comfortable if the Final Judgment happened right now?

Again, the Spirit may speak to you in ways that differ from what is listed above. The important thing is to let the message of James "induct" us into the perfect will of God. Though the conviction of the Spirit can be unpleasant at times, it promises to produce good fruit in our lives (Gal. 5:22-23).

☩ ⟨χ⟩DISCIPLE

The spiritual challenges of James in this section are difficult, but the consequences of ignoring God's will can be even more difficult. The **Disciple** step is all about taking concrete steps to do God's Word in the here and now. Please consider making a personal covenant with the challenges of James 5:1-9 by committing to do the following:

This week, I covenant to . . .

- Deny myself some material pleasure and replace it with a gift to help those in need.

- Look for at least one, concrete situation where I can be a clear voice for justice and fairness.

- Alleviate, in real terms, the pain of those who have suffered at the hands of the rich and powerful.

If the spiritual mandates of James in this section prove to be daunting for the individual, discipling others in this regard can be even more challenging. This kind of intense mentoring has the best chance of success within the context of very close relationships, like a good marriage or healthy family environment. Apart from these contexts, the opportunity to disciple others in the counsel of James 5:1-9 may prove to be a once-in-a-lifetime experience. Nevertheless, when that opportunity does come along, we need to be ready to stand for what's right, regardless of the cost.

As you proceed to the next and final lesson of this study on James, you will notice that as James brings his faith-filled burden to a close, in a real sense, his thoughts come full circle. That is, he begins to reflect again on the important themes of trials, patience, and prayer. It was these topics that formed the opening of his epistle (1:2-7), and it is these subjects that comprise its closing (5:10-18). So in finishing this IBS on James, we will be returning to its beginning. That is how it should be—an ever-continuing reflection on this great book of the Bible.

A PENTECOSTAL APPROACH
to
BIBLE STUDY

LESSON TEN

James

5:10-20

REAL FAITH
BELIEVES IN PRAYER

LESSON TEN

James 5:10-20

Real Faith Believes in Prayer

 ## KEY VERSE

My brothers, if one of you should wander from the truth and someone should bring him back, [20] remember this: Whoever turns a sinner from the error of his way will save him from death and cover over a multitude of sins (James 5:19-20).

Introduction

These two verses capture the entire vision of James. All of his warnings and prophetic exhortations were intended to bring back those who had wandered from the truth. His burning zeal was to turn sinners from their error so they could escape the certain fate of death (1:15). All of his pleadings, though harsh at times, were to bring God's atoning grace to bear upon the sin problem so that innumerable sins might be "covered."

In this last section, James recaps all of the major themes he has addressed in his epistle. In a real sense, James is summarizing everything he has said thus far. So as you study this last section in James, allow your mind to recall all of the fine points the apostle has presented throughout his epistle.

Indeed, as we prepare to arrive at the end of our journey in James, we should pause for prayer. In particular, we should ask for the Spirit's help in making the life-imparting message of James real in our lives. James would have it no other way.

PAUSE *for* PRAYER

If James has taught us anything, he has taught us that we are utterly dependent on God. He has taught us that without the help of the Spirit, we cannot rightly follow the path to discipleship. Yet it is this kind of knowledge that lies at the heart of true spirituality. Thus the psalmist prays, "Show me your ways, O Lord, teach me your paths; guide me in your truth and teach me, for you are God my Savior, and my hope is in you all day long" (Ps. 25:4-5). Let this be your prayer as you work through this final chapter. Pray that God reveal His ways, that He teach you His paths, and that He guide you in His truth.

THE TEXT

James 5:10-20

[10]Brothers, as an example of patience in the face of suffering, take the prophets who spoke in the name of the Lord. [11] As you know, we consider blessed those who have persevered. You have heard of Job's

perseverance and have seen what the Lord finally brought about. The Lord is full of compassion and

mercy. [12] Above all, my brothers, do not swear—not by heaven or by earth or by anything else. Let your

"Yes" be yes, and your "No," no, or you will be condemned. [13] Is any one of you in trouble? He should

pray. Is anyone happy? Let him sing songs of praise. [14] Is any one of you sick? He should call the elders of

the church to pray over him and anoint him with oil in the name of the Lord. [15] And the prayer offered

in faith will make the sick person well; the Lord will raise him up. If he has sinned, he will be forgiven. [16]

Therefore confess your sins to each other and pray for each other so that you may be healed. The prayer

of a righteous man is powerful and effective. [17] Elijah was a man just like us. He prayed earnestly that

it would not rain, and it did not rain on the land for three and a half years. [18] Again he prayed, and the

heavens gave rain, and the earth produced its crops. [19] My brothers, if one of you should wander from the truth and someone should bring him back, [20] remember this: Whoever turns a sinner from the

error of his way will save him from death and cover over a multitude of sins.

DISCOVER

James has saved the best for last. That is, there are many echoes and references to the Old Testament in this final section of his epistle. Your task here is to craft some select Helping Questions to draw out the rich connections that James has made to the prophets of old. As always, be on the lookout for the contemporary lessons we can learn from these references to the prophets. In fact, the very first verse of this lesson, James 5:10, explicitly speaks of the patience that the prophets demonstrated in the face of suffering.

Again, as you *dis*-cover the facts contained in this section, remember that James is summarizing most of the main points that he has already made in his epistle. So look for the connections between what James says in 5:10-20 and with what he has already shared with his readers.

As usual, some sample questions are supplied here to get you oriented to the task at hand.

Sample Helping Questions

- How might James' exhortation to patience in the midst of trial (5:10-11) relate to what he has already said in 1:2-3?

ANSWER

- Where else in his epistle has James mentioned the compassion and mercy of the Lord?

ANSWER

• What words of Jesus might James have in mind in James 1:12?

ANSWER

Now use your experience in creating Helping Questions to "pry out" the remaining facts of James 5:10-20.

MY HELPING QUESTIONS AND ANSWERS

MY HELPING QUESTIONS AND ANSWERS CONTINUED

In case you have not used these questions, here are a couple more:

* How might the final reward of Job (James 5:11) relate to James' emphasis on the rewards the saints will receive at the Second Coming?

ANSWER

- How do the words of James in 5:13 contrast with what he has already said in 1:13-16?

ANSWER

Now review all of your Helping Questions and answers and write out all of the facts that you have *un*-covered. (Do you still remember the literal meaning of the Greek word *alētheia* in James 5:10-20?) Write out your findings in the space provided.

MY FINDINGS

MY FINDINGS CONTINUED

DISCERN

As you apply your marking system to James 5:10-20, you will notice that many words are repeated, especially words concerning prayer. So you will need to give special attention to highlighting important words like these. You will notice, too, that a good portion of this passage speaks of "sickness" and "healing." So you will need to find a way to develop contrasting symbols or colors that reflect sickness on the one hand and healing on the other. So take your time to create a good marking system that highlights all of the special words and features contained in this portion of James.

Yet before you do, you should seek God's guidance in understanding these final words of James. After all, something would be amiss to be studying a section that emphasizes prayer, yet we do not even pray about the interpretation!

PAUSE *for* PRAYER

In 5:11, James refers to Job, and describes him as an extraordinary example of being patient in the midst of trial. Unlike those who blamed God for their trials and temptations (James 1:13-15), Job refused to do so (Job 13:15). Yet there is another aspect of Job that can help us understand James. Job was a man who prayed great prayers. In Job 16:19-21 we read, "Even now my witness is in heaven; my advocate is on high. My intercessor is my friend as my eyes pour out tears to God; on behalf of a man he pleads with God as a man pleads for his friend." What an amazing prayer! It seems that long before the incarnation and ascension of Christ, Job had a vision of the Lord's intercession for us (see also Heb. 7:25; Rom 8:34). Job may even be speaking of the intercession of the Holy Spirit long before the Day of Pentecost (see Acts 2:4; Rom. 8:26-27). Even so, as we enter into this important study on prayer, we need to appeal to the intercession of both the Son and the Spirit.

The following comments will help you in the development and application of your Helping Tools:

- James 5:10-20 grants us rare insight into the worship experiences of the early church. Be sure to create some memorable symbols that represent the singing of songs, the offering of praise, laying on of hands, and the anointing with oil (5:13-14).

- Recall that the word *confess* in 5:16 literally means "to say the same thing" or "to agree with God."

- Once again, James speaks about elements that can be found in nature, such as rain, soil and crops. In past lessons, you have probably used symbols to represent these features and you should use these same symbols here again.

Continue to "brainstorm" about ways that you can note important features and themes in James 5:10-20. All of this work, as you know, will serve you well when you write out your own interpretation.

➡PULLING IT ALL TOGETHER⬅

It is time to review all the facts that have emerged as a result of the Helping Questions and the insights that have been *un*-covered by your Helping Tools. Again, take special care in studying the patterns, emphases, and contrasts made evident by your Helping Tools. Jot down some of the interpretive ideas that you see as a result of your work.

The following points will guide your thoughts as you seek to combine and coordinate everything that has come to light in this passage:

- How might the "prayer of faith" (5:15 KJV) relate to the "good and perfect gifts coming down from the Father of lights" (see 1:17)?

ANSWER

ANSWER CONTINUED

- Where else in the Scriptures do you read about anointing with oil (5:14)?

ANSWER

- What kind of connections do you think James wants us to draw between the experiences of prayer, faith, and the forgiveness of sins (see 5:13-16)?

ANSWER

- Why does James cite the person and experience of Elijah in 5:17?

ANSWER

Now you should integrate all of your findings and write out your interpretation in the space provided.

MY INTERPRETATION

DEVOTE

There is so much in this passage that calls out to us as believers. For example, James would have us to patiently endure periods of stress and trial. In the place of exaggeration and wild claims, James says that our "yes" should simply be yes and our "no" should simply be no. And most of all, James exhorts us to be effectual in prayer. Indeed, these are the "big things" of our Christian life—things that we need to continually pray about. Now is one of those times that the Spirit is calling us to prayer.

PAUSE for PRAYER

One of the most dramatic stories in the life of Jesus was the desperate plea of a father for his son. This story is found in Mark 9:17-27. The father is struggling to believe that Jesus can, in fact, restore his son to full mental and spiritual health. In response, the Scriptures state, "Jesus said unto him, If thou canst believe, all things *are* possible to him that believeth. And straightway the father of the child cried out, and said with tears, Lord, I believe; help thou mine unbelief" (Mark 9:23-24 KJV). The point here is that even if we do not have perfect faith, that does not mean our prayers will go unanswered. So, as you seek to respond to James' call in these scriptures, act on the faith that you have in order that God might grant you even more faith.

The following questions are designed to help you commit to a higher level of faith in the Lord.

- What types of trials quickly exhaust your patience?

- Do you feel confident in just giving your word, or do you have to resort to swearing in an attempt to get people to believe you?

- When in trouble, is your first impulse to pray?

- When you are happy, do you, without thinking, begin to sing praises to the Lord?

- When sick, do you have the faith to believe that the Lord can heal you by the laying on of hands and the anointing with oil?

Again, it may seem strange to pray about praying, but this is just what James is leading us to do. Jot down some of your thoughts in your journal about prayer. Revisit them from time to time and prayerfully review them. Be aware of God's personal voice to you as you pray about praying.

⁘ DISCIPLE

The kinds of spiritual commitments made in the **Devote** step require concrete action if they are to have any real meaning in our lives. Indeed, if James were to read your journal, more than likely his first response would be, "You have done well by making such fine commitments to the Lord. Now, what are you going to do about it?" And this is what the **Devote** step is all about: acting upon our covenant with the Word. The following comments are to help you make the spiritual mandates of James 5:10-20 become real in your life.

This week, in the light of what I have learned in James 5:10-20, I will . . .

- Let my "yes" be yes and my "no" be no. That is, I will not resort to swearing to get my point across.

- Not take matters into my own hands when encountering trials and difficulties. Rather, I will turn to faith, prayer, praise, and the spiritual gifts working through others to meet the challenges of life.

- Refuse to be defensive when I am in the wrong. That is, I will confess my faults to those concerned and seek to receive their forgiveness.

With regard to discipling others, the final words of James 5:19-20 relate to the entire epistle. That is, all of the teachings found in James can be used to redirect those who have wandered from the faith. The entire goal of making disciples is to turn sinners from their errors, direct them toward salvation, deliver them from death, and, by God's grace, be instrumental in covering a multitude of sins.

Let this be your standing prayer as you come to the end of your journey in James. Pray that God grant you "the Spirit of wisdom and revelation" (Eph 1:17) so that you may fulfill the Great Commission (Matt 28:19-20) and lead many on the *path to discipleship*.

CONCLUDING REMARKS

James

Concluding Remarks

When writing to the Philippians, Paul states, "For it is God who works in you to will and to act according to his good purpose" (Phil. 2:13). This biblical truth is both mysterious and marvelous at the same time! In some way, the Spirit is able to inspire us not only to choose God's perfect will, but also to do God's perfect will. This means that God has been intimately involved in your choice to study *James: A Path to Discipleship*. So in one sense, you are to be commended for completing an in-depth IBS of James. Yet on a deeper level, you have completed a spiritual journey that was initiated by God, directed by God, and brought to completion by God. This means that everything you have learned and experienced in this study of James has been "according to His good purpose." This fact alone is enough for us to pause and ask, "What have I learned and experienced in my study of *James: A Path to Discipleship*?"

In answering this question, you might want to review the following list. It contains some of the major themes and spiritual challenges that you have encountered in your study of James. As you read through this list, reflect on your journey through James. Take stock of where you were spiritually prior to beginning this study, and compare that to where you are now in the Lord. What kinds of spiritual growth have you experienced as a result of your study of James? What kinds of change have you undergone by accepting the challenges set forth in the **Devote** and **Disciple** steps of IBS? To what extent have you come closer to "making disciples of all nations" (see Matt. 28:19) by not only knowing the teachings in James, but also by doing what James teaches?

11 CONCLUDING REMARKS

By prayerfully reflecting on the following list and honestly answering questions like the ones above, you are preparing yourself for the wrap-up session on James. This final lesson will give you an opportunity to share with your study group the kinds of growth you have experienced in studying James. And if you have completed *James: A Path to Discipleship* on your own, a period of reflection and self-examination will prove to be invaluable. It will clarify all of the wonderful truths that God has revealed to you in the process of studying His Word. Also, recalling what you have learned will sharpen your resolve to follow through on your covenant with the Word of God in James.

Major themes encountered in James include:

- The true source of temptation and sin
- The proper Christian response to temptation
- The inestimable value of a mature, stable faith
- A proper Christian perspective on wealth and materialism
- God is the source of every good gift.
- God has chosen the poor of this world to be rich in faith.
- Jesus is coming again and there will be a final judgment.
- Friendship with the world means that you are an enemy of God.
- There is a wisdom that comes from God.
- God hears and answers our prayers.
- God is merciful.
- God heals and forgives sins.

Spiritual challenges set forth in James include:

- Be patient under trial and temptation.

- Tame the wildly sinful nature of human speech.

- Actualize your faith in godly works and conduct.

- Don't show favoritism.

- Don't be wise in your own eyes.

- Put an end to selfishness.

- Be fair and just in business and finance.

- Don't use swear words.

- Be merciful to those who have fallen from grace. You too may need such mercy one day.

In preparing for the final wrap-up session, you may want to write out your thoughts in your journal or logbook. Writing things down has a way of helping us to be intentional in our work. That is, it helps us to coordinate our thoughts, and in the process, it helps to fix God's Word in our minds.

As you prepare to conclude your study of James, I pray that the words of the apostle Paul would become real in your life. When writing to the Colossians, he prayed: "Let the word of Christ dwell in you richly as you teach and admonish one another with all wisdom, and as you sing psalms, hymns and spiritual songs with gratitude in your hearts to God. And whatever you do, whether in word or deed, do it all in the name of the Lord Jesus, giving thanks to God the Father through him" (Col. 3:16-17). Amen.

About the Author

William A. Simmons, professor of New Testament Studies and Greek at Lee University, Cleveland, Tennessee, received his Ph.D. from the University of St. Andrews in Scotland. Bill's specialty is New Testament exegesis with a concentration in the Pauline Epistles and Koine Greek. His published works include *Peoples of the New Testament World: An Illustrated Guide; A Concise Background of the New Testament; Paul and Jesus: A Theology of Inclusion; New Testament Survey;* and a commentary on Galatians. Bill has also published several articles in the *Evangelical Dictionary of New Testament Theology* and the Lexham Project for Logos Bible Software. He has also done teaching and mission work at the European Bible Seminary in Rudersburg, Germany, and taught in other countries such as Korea, Honduras, the Philippines, Guatemala, Scotland, Cuba, and Peru. His hobbies include outdoor sports and woodworking. Bill resides in Cleveland, Tennessee with his wife, Lenae, and has three children: David, Nathaniel, and Laura.